PUBLISHING
JOURNAL
ARTICLES

SUCCESS IN RESEARCH

The Success in Research series has been designed by Cindy Becker and Pam Denicolo to provide short, authoritative and accessible guides for students, researchers and academics on the key area of professional and research development.

Each book is written with an eye to avoiding jargon and each aims to cut to the chase of what readers really need to know about a given topic. These are practical and supportive books and will be essential reading for any students or researchers interested in developing their skills and broadening their professional and methodological knowledge in an academic context.

SUCCESS IN RESEARCH

PUBLISHING JOURNAL ARTICLES

LUCINDA BECKER ♀ PAM DENICOLO

Los Angeles | London | New Delhi
Singapore | Washington DC

First published 2012

SAGE Publications Ltd
1 Oliver's Yard
55 City Road
London EC1Y 1SP

SAGE Publications Inc.
2455 Teller Road
Thousand Oaks, California 91320

SAGE Publications India Pvt Ltd
B 1/I 1 Mohan Cooperative Industrial Area
Mathura Road
New Delhi 110 044

SAGE Publications Asia-Pacific Pte Ltd
3 Church Street
#10-04 Samsung Hub
Singapore 049483

Library of Congress Control Number: 2011932458

British Library Cataloguing in Publication data

A catalogue record for this book is available from the British Library

ISBN 978-1-4462-0062-9
ISBN 978-1-4462-0063-6 (pbk)

Typeset by C&M Digitals (P) Ltd, Chennai, India
Printed in Great Britain by CPI Group (UK) Ltd, Croydon, CR0 4YY
Printed on paper from sustainable resources

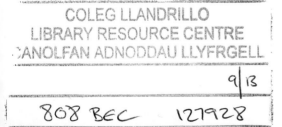

This book is dedicated to all the research students and colleagues who have been so generous in telling us about their endeavours and sharing their tribulations and triumphs so honestly. A community of scholars is a wonderful thing.

CONTENTS

About the authors   ix

1 When, what and where to publish   **1**
Why are you going to write an article?   2
When should you write an article?   8
What should you publish?   12
Where should you place an article?   18

2 Selecting your topic/adapting your work   **28**
Selecting your topic   28
Adapting your work   30

3 Planning and getting started   **42**
Spider charts   46
Flow charts   51
Brainstorms   53
Mind mapping   56

4 Coping with writer's block   **59**

5 Getting the style right   **73**
Your writing style   73
If you are writing in your second language   74
The structure of your article   75
The abstract   75
The introduction   77
The article on the page   78
Signposting and structure   79

Presenting technical data   80
Textual options   81
Concluding your article   81
The language of your article   82
Your readership   82
Writing simply   84
Improving your style   85
Editing your article   86
Polishing your article   89

6   Learning how to stop writing your article   95
Why you need to stop   95
Why you cannot seem to stop   97
Learning how to stop   101
And then not really stopping   103

7   Working with editors and reviewers   108

8   Recovering from rejection   119
Telling people   120
Prepare for rejection   122
Use the reviews   124
Make a plan of action   128

9   Intellectual property rights   129

Some final thoughts   138
Further reading   139
Index   141

ABOUT THE AUTHORS

Dr Lucinda Becker, an award winning Senior Lecturer and Teaching Fellow in the Department of English Language and Literature at the University of Reading, has spent her career committed to enhancing the skills of under-graduates and research postgraduates. She has written numerous successful study skills guides for students. As a professional trainer she also works through-out the United Kingdom and Europe, devising and delivering training in communication and management techniques, principally to lawyers, engineers and scientists.

Professor Pam Denicolo, a chartered constructivist psychologist, found her early research commitment to generally improving learning and teaching in Higher Education focusing progressively on the needs of graduate students, their supervisors and other professionals seeking to develop their practice. Her passion for supporting graduate students and other early career researchers is demonstrated through her numerous successful doctoral candidates and her leading roles in national and international organisations such as the UK Council for Graduate Education, the International Study Association on Teachers and Teaching, the Society for Research into Higher Education Postgraduate Network, the Impact and Evaluation Group and other working groups of Vitae, and the QAA Doctoral Characteristics Advisory Group, all of which have resulted in many publications, presentations and workshops.

Cindy and Pam worked exuberantly together for many years managing and developing the Graduate School at the University of Reading and providing a substantial contribution to its Research Methods, Generic Skills and Doctoral Supervisor training.

1

WHEN, WHAT AND WHERE TO PUBLISH

CHAPTER OVERVIEW

This chapter will be especially helpful if:

- You are unsure about whether or not to produce an article at this stage in your research career.
- People have offered you a mass of advice, some of it contradictory, and you want to sort through it in deciding how best to approach an article.
- You want to produce an article but feel unsure about the most productive way to approach the material.
- You are nervous about the whole process of writing an article.

As you begin to read this book, we feel that we know you a little. You are interested in writing an article for a journal – that is presumably why you are reading it. We also know that you are not especially interested in doing this the hard way, by trial and error, but would rather take the most direct route to success. So, you want to learn the craft of writing journal articles and use the advice in this guide to achieve this. You also know a little about us: you will probably have scrutinised the back cover and table of contents of this book before you started to read, so you know who we are and how we are approaching this subject.

What we cannot know about each other, just yet, is the approach we would all take to writing journal articles. You will learn about our approach as you read on, and at the same time you will be devising your own strategies, taking the advice from this book where you feel you need it. You may simply skim read some sections (you might not, for example, be suffering from writer's block) whilst others will be beside you as you plan, form and write your article.

We cannot know how far you are along your journey to a completed article. Perhaps you have submitted an article in the past and not been successful, or you might have several articles published but want help with one aspect of the process which you find burdensome. You may well, of course, be facing the challenge of writing your very first journal article. It is for this reason that we have structured this book so as to take you from the very first stage of the process right through to the end of your article and beyond. We might not be your constant companions on the journey, but we hope that you will return to the book again and again as each new challenge arises.

What we do not need to know about you is your specific situation. This guide has been designed to support any scholar who is interested in this field, whether you are a research student in the early stages, or a more experienced postgraduate, whether you are an early career researcher or an academic with far more experience. Indeed, you might not be in academia at all. We refer throughout to supervisors and mentors. You might have a doctoral supervisor, you might have a research mentor, but really we mean here anyone who you feel is offering you advice on your development as a researcher, and this could be several people in your life. The examples we have used have been drawn from many disciplines and the advice is relevant to writers regardless of their first language or the location of their institution.

It is worth us pointing out at the outset that, whilst our focus in this guide is on helping you to produce a successful article, it will soon become clear to you that the advice we offer is relevant well beyond this task. Many forms of writing require you to work through the stages we outline throughout this book, so you may find that you return to it repeatedly, in writing research bids, producing a book chapter or monograph, preparing a conference paper, indeed, whenever you are required to disseminate your research through the written word.

The first question to ask yourself is, funnily enough, the one most easily and often overlooked. Why do you want to write a journal article? It may seem like asking the obvious – of course you want, and need, to become a published scholar – but your motivation for writing will have a significant effect upon the early stages of your journey. You need to be clear about why you are writing so that you can ensure that you end up in the right place, with the right article, at the right time.

WHY ARE YOU GOING TO WRITE AN ARTICLE?

If you spend a little time now considering your reasons for writing an article you will be able to take control of the situation and move ahead effectively. We have listed below some of the most common motivations for beginning on a journal article, and then we offer you some advice on each situation.

- You have been told that a chapter or essay would make a good article.
- You think it will advance your academic career.
- You hope it will help your career outside academia.
- Everyone else seems to do it.
- You want your ideas to reach a wider audience.
- You hope to increase your academic network.
- You enjoy writing.

It may be that several of these factors have come together to make writing a journal article seem like the next logical step in your career as a scholar. Let us look at each in turn.

YOU HAVE BEEN TOLD THAT A CHAPTER OR ESSAY WOULD MAKE A GOOD ARTICLE

This is an exciting position to be in, having work which you produced with no thought of publication being considered as worthy of publication. You will, naturally, feel flattered that it is so admired and you will want to get on with publishing it. This may be the best option, of course, but you are unlikely to be able simply to send off your piece and expect it to be snapped up by a journal publisher. There are advantages and challenges to this situation, and a clear way forward:

ADVANTAGES

The work already exists, so you are not starting from scratch, which could make the process easier. In reality, although this will rightly boost your confidence, you will still have challenges to face.

CHALLENGES

Because the work already exists in one form (as a chapter of your dissertation or thesis, for example) it can be far more difficult than you might expect to convert it into an article. Your readership is going to be different and it will be read out of its original context, so you will need to turn it into a free standing article rather than an embedded piece of writing.

MOVING ON

Although you have the advantage of material which you have already written, you will need to deconstruct the work, identifying the salient points and reworking them to create an article which is fit for purpose.

GETTING HELP

You will find the sections on adapting your work in the next chapter especially useful.

YOU THINK IT WILL ADVANCE YOUR ACADEMIC CAREER

And why should you not think this? We hear all the time about the importance of publishing within academia, and it is certainly taken as a measure of research success. Much of the funding for any institution comes from forms of research assessment which rely on publications as an indication of research activity.

ADVANTAGES

Publication of a journal article will get your name out there and so will increase your standing in the academic community. It will therefore be a benefit to your career.

CHALLENGES

In an environment under ever increasing funding pressure, you absolutely must ensure that you are publishing at the right time for you, and in the right place. You will need to analyse how much time you can dedicate to writing an article amongst all of the other competing demands on your time and prioritise it accordingly. You also must, absolutely must, seek advice. Your article, and so your reputation, will be judged not only on its content, but also on where it is published, and this is going to be vital if you are to get the maximum benefit for your efforts.

MOVING ON

Seek support and guidance from your supervisor or mentor, from your colleagues, from any research advisory board within your institution. Make sure that you are perfectly clear about the benefits of publication before you begin to write the article itself.

GETTING HELP

Before you seek advice you will probably want to have an idea of what you might publish. The early chapters of this guide will help you in this, and we would recommend that you do not go beyond the early planning stages before you work on the placement of your article. It makes much more sense to write with a target journal in mind than to write it and then have to adapt the work at a later stage.

YOU HOPE IT WILL HELP YOUR CAREER OUTSIDE ACADEMIA

In some ways you are on safer ground here. If you are already working in a professional area with which you are familiar, you are likely to be fully aware of the type of publication you need to target, and the benefits which will accrue from publishing an article in your field.

ADVANTAGES

You know your area, the competition might be a little less fierce in trying to place your article (depending upon your professional area) and you can be clear about your target readership.

CHALLENGES

If you are aiming at a profession subsequent to your academic research, rather than working in it already, you will need to carry out the same level of research as we have suggested above, so that you can guarantee that you are targeting the best journal for your ambitions and your research area.

MOVING ON

Your focus cannot be entirely on your research: you will need to spend time assessing the market in professional journals in your field to see what might appeal to that readership. It may be more likely that you will have to focus on just one aspect of just one part of your research and work it up into an article which will be of greatest interest to your chosen readership.

GETTING HELP

The support within academia will be the same as above, your supervisor or mentor, your research colleagues and so on, but you will also need support from your profession. Canvas the widest possible range of opinion from those you think will have the 'inside information' on where and what to publish.

EVERYONE ELSE SEEMS TO DO IT

It can sometimes seem as if scholars are constantly writing articles, throwing them off at a moment's notice every day of the academic week. This is just not the case. We think that the ratio of article talked about as being 'in the pipeline' as compared to those actually written, let alone published, is at least four to one. So, you are going to have to cut through the mythology and find out what is really happening in your area of expertise. In some areas and within some institutions, for example, it is far more common to produce full texts, either monographs (single authored books) or jointly published volumes, than articles. In other areas, articles are the norm.

ADVANTAGES

If you find that it is the case that articles are the most usual route to publication in your field, and that there are many of them published each year, this could mean that you have fertile ground for your publication, with plenty of journals being published in your area, all of which need to include articles.

(Continued)

(Continued)

CHALLENGES

These are an obvious corollary of the advantages: many eager scholars clamouring to find publishers could mean stiff competition.

MOVING ON

You will have to be astute about the approach that you take. However mainstream your research area, be prepared to be adaptable in order to produce an article which might not reflect the main body of your research, but which will capture the imagination of journal editors.

GETTING HELP

Your greatest source of help, beyond this guide, will be the journals themselves. Researching each journal and reading copious back copies will give you a good feel not only for what topics and approaches have been popular in the past, but also give you a good feel for the current direction of the journal. This can seem like a time-consuming distraction, but it is a far better use of your time than simply writing an article and then waiting in vain for someone to publish it.

YOU WANT YOUR IDEAS TO REACH A WIDER AUDIENCE

This is perhaps the most natural reason for wanting to write an article: dissemination is the natural instinct of most scholars, and it provides a powerful motivation to write and be published.

ADVANTAGES

Your motivation will be high and you will enjoy following the guidance in this book as a way to increase your effectiveness and chances of publication. Your natural research excitement should come through in your writing.

CHALLENGES

In your enthusiasm for disseminating your ideas, you might overburden your article with every single research idea you have. This will inevitably lead to a cramped and superficial article, even if you are in the early stages of your research career.

MOVING ON

Whilst you can give yourself fairly free rein to let your passion for your research show through at the writing stage of the process, try to curb your excitement a little in the early stages, as you plan your article and select material.

GETTING HELP

It can be difficult to assess how much material would make for a good article unless you have plenty of experience, and it can be demoralising and difficult to have to reduce the content of an article significantly once it has been written. Use the planning advice in this book to produce a communication platform. Discuss your plan in detail with those around you, aiming to cut the ideas down to a size and shape which fits the journal you have in mind. Although seeing your article in print is going to be a thrill regardless of where it is published, try not to stint on the time you spend researching journals: your work deserves the best possible showcase.

YOU HOPE TO INCREASE YOUR ACADEMIC NETWORK

In this respect, journal articles can work in a similar way to giving papers or presentations at conferences: fellow scholars from all over the world may contact you as a result, and you can increase your academic network significantly in this way.

ADVANTAGES

You will increase your network, and if this is your primary aim you need to ensure that the topic on which you publish is one in which you have a 'live', active interest, rather than one which you worked on some time ago and which is of only limited relevance to your current research activity.

CHALLENGES

You will need to strive to create an 'open' article, one which raises questions and thought provoking challenges in the readers. If you appear simply to be trying to offer the 'last word' in an area (impossible in any case in reality) you are less likely to invite comment and so will not boost your academic network as much as you might have hoped.

MOVING ON

This need not be a great challenge, as long as you remember in the planning stages to introduce an 'open' aspect to your article.

GETTING HELP

Conferences, research seminars and symposia can help here. If you are happy to present an early version of your article to your colleagues and fellow researchers, you will get a good idea of how lively the response to your article will be.

YOU ENJOY WRITING

It is hard to fault a love of writing as a reason to produce a journal article: you have an enjoyable and satisfying time ahead of you!

ADVANTAGES

It is surprising how many scholars actually do not especially enjoy the process of writing, so if you know that you are not one of them you have an automatic advantage when it comes to crafting a journal article.

CHALLENGES

Your natural love of writing can lead you astray dramatically. What starts out as a journal article can rapidly become an embryonic monograph almost without you noticing.

MOVING ON

You must exert a strict discipline over yourself. However much you enjoy writing, and however much you are convinced that your potential readers would be interested in a fascinating point you are making, a journal article presents a restricted space in which to write. You must plan meticulously and (perhaps more challengingly) you must stick firmly to your plan, regardless of temptation.

GETTING HELP

Focus on the planning chapters of this book before you go on to study in any detail the sections on writing. If you find that you simply cannot seem to stay within a word count, try introducing another stage in the process. Take your plan and expand it to the full article, but only in bullet points. Then expand each bullet point into beautiful writing, but refuse to allow yourself to introduce even one single extra piece of information.

WHEN SHOULD YOU WRITE AN ARTICLE?

The obvious initial response to this question is *now*. You have decided that you want to write an article. You feel that you should be aiming for publication. You have bought this book, so is that not the only possible answer to the question? You are probably right to answer 'now'. It takes an inordinate amount of time for an article to go from writing to publication and your academic reputation, perhaps your career advancement, relies on you publishing. We spend much of our lives urging our research students to get out there and share their work with the world, fully aware of the pitfalls of ignoring this important aspect of the life of a scholar. If you are aware that you have already left it a little later than you had hoped, or if you are being strongly advised by your supervisor or mentor to begin the process, then you need do nothing more than plunge into this guide and begin on the road to an article. However, if you feel, having taken advice, that you have some leeway as to when to start on your next, or perhaps your first, article, then this checklist might help you.

Before you take the plunge

1 Putting aside any everyday moans and groans about overwork, do you have time to begin on an article right now?
2 Are there no other competing demands upon your attention which you feel would harm your work if they were neglected a little in favour of writing an article?
3 Does your subject area tend to favour articles over books as the most desirable form of publication?
4 Do you have the germ of an idea, and some research material to support it, which you feel would make a good article?
5 Do you have a good sense of where you can most advantageously submit your article for publication?
6 Do you know the best way to approach your chosen journal? Does it offer guidance on this (either in the journal itself or on its website) and are you clear about how to approach it? If not, can your supervisor or mentor offer guidance on this?
7 Do you tend to write in short bursts, mulling your thoughts over in between periods of writing?

If you have answered 'yes' to all of these questions, you are ready to go and can happily read on, knowing that this is a good time to begin your article. If you have answered 'no' to any of the questions, it does not necessarily mean that you should not go ahead now, but it would be worth reading our guidance below first:

1 I do not have the time to write an article now

The good news is that very few academics feel they have the time to produce an article right now – ever. Yet they have to do it, so how? The secret is to assume that there will never be a perfect time to set aside the space to write an article, and then focus on how you work best. If you are happy to devote the time to planning an article, it is then possible to write it in small sections, allowing yourself just an hour or so for each writing session. This is often advocated nowadays as the most productive way for academics to write. However, if you know that this simply would not work for you, you will need to plan your time so that you can move around your research and other commitments until you reach the point where you can allow yourself enough time to concentrate simply on writing, and you will blank this time out firmly in your diary. This may put off the moment when you actually begin to write, but it will ensure that you can write with total concentration and at some speed once you begin.

2 It will harm my research progress if I take time to write an article now

This is a similar concern to the one expressed above, but suggests that you have analysed your situation and come to a studied conclusion about your commitments, rather than simply suffering from the crowded timetables under which many academics labour on a daily basis. Before you abandon the idea of writing an article altogether, work with your supervisor or mentor to ensure that your perception is, indeed, correct. In this way you can postpone writing an article safe in the knowledge that you are doing the right thing. Of course, the secret to success in these circumstances is to postpone the challenge rather than abandoning it altogether. Before you know it, several months will have slid by, so make sure that you have a deadline for coming back and revisiting the question of when you should begin.

3 Writing a book would be a more advantageous aim in my discipline

It is never safe to assume that this is the case simply on the basis of casual conversations or a general 'feel' for your area. You will need to investigate this as thoroughly as possible, at the very least by talking to your supervisor or mentor and your head of department or school. If it does genuinely seem to be the case that you should focus your energy on producing a full text, you might find yourself in a conundrum. It may be that you will not be in a position to produce a full-length monograph until much later in your research, so consider instead the option of contributing to a joint authored publication, in which case much of the advice offered in this guide will be of relevance to you. Do also make sure that you keep an eye on the situation: it may change and you will need to be ready to change your writing strategy in line with developments.

4 I do not have an idea, or enough material, for an article

This is so unlikely to be the case that we feel we can almost dismiss it out of hand. Except, of course, that it is a very real concern for many facing their first article and so we want to address with you the potential difference between your perception and the probable reality. Good journal articles rely upon a good idea, based on a sound premise which can be supported by reliable evidence. That is all. If you look at it in this way, you will find that you already have all of these things in place.

Having spent many years working with researchers we have learnt that the first of these, a good idea and a sound premise, are the key elements in article writing. You may have to spend a little time after making an initial plan gathering up more evidence or ordering the information that you have in order to show how well it supports your idea, but the fact that you will have collected and analysed less evidence than a scholar with many years' more experience does not disqualify you from writing an excellent article; it simply means that your article may have a narrower focus, and will not suffer at all from that.

If we have not yet convinced you, we hope you will be inspired by the next chapter of this guide, which will demonstrate for you the different ways in which you might find your ideas and how to work them up into an article.

5 I do not know where best to try to place an article

This is common to most scholars when they approach the challenge of writing an article, and it is a good reason to pause for a while. Until you know the journal and readership at which you are targeting your article, it can be disadvantageous to jump in. By doing the research (some of which is outlined in the next section of this chapter) you will not only get a better idea of how to nuance your article towards a particular readership, you will also be exposing yourself to the style of writing in different journals, and this is going to be useful to you once you actually start to write up the article. So, a pause here is appropriate, but a complete full stop is not. Do the research, find the right journal, and you are ready to move ahead.

6 I do not tend to write in short bursts and leave time to think between writing sessions; I prefer to produce a piece all in one go

There are two distinct types of writer: those who enjoy mulling over an article for many months, occasionally writing a paragraph or two and never feeling (or assiduously ignoring) any pressure to complete it, and those who would find this an almost unbearable, tedious and counter-productive approach. It is vital, at this early stage, that you know which sort of writer you are. Thinking back to your previous experiences will help. Most of us tend to know whether we love the excitement of deadlines or always complete significantly before them, whether we enjoy late night writing so as to get something finished or would prefer to rest and begin again the next day, whether we tend to rely on adrenaline to get us through each challenge or would rather try to eliminate that aspect of the process.

If you are the former, a long-haul writer, you need to start as soon as possible so as to give yourself time to produce your article. Once it is complete you can be confident that it is the best you can achieve, having spent so long considering the topic, although there is a chance that you might never actually get around to finishing it. If you are the latter, a sprint writer, you run the risk of writing in such a rush that you will miss out salient points and not spot the omissions before you submit, so in your case we would advise you to delay writing until you have formed a painstaking plan and reviewed and revised it several times, just to ensure that you can write at speed and with confidence.

WHAT SHOULD YOU PUBLISH?

You may already have a clear idea about the topic of your article and you may even have some draft material in place, but now is a good time to look anew at what, exactly, you plan to cover. This can seem simple, but the source of your material is often as important as the topic area at this stage of the process.

You will probably already have used and reused some of your material, perhaps by writing a draft chapter for your thesis and also covering similar material in a conference paper. You will also have material which has only been written up by you once, and some research which is little more than notes on findings. All academics live their lives in this state of flux: gathering, analysing, drawing some early conclusions, writing up a little, leaving some work alone to simmer whilst your mind ticks over, thinking about its implications. This is a good position to be in, as you can make creative choices about your source material for an article.

Our main injunction here would be to avoid the obvious, just for the moment, whilst you consider the advantages and disadvantages of the source material to which you might turn for your article. It is so easy (for researchers and their mentors alike) to simply assume that the best way to approach this is to rework a chapter of your dissertation or thesis. This might be the case, but it can also throw up more problems than solutions, so we outline here a range of options open to you, so that you can consider your best approach before you move on.

A word on terminology here: the terms 'dissertation' and 'thesis' can mean different things in different countries and between institutions. When we refer to a dissertation, we mean a substantial piece of written up research, perhaps 20,000 to 30,000 words in length and typically produced at master's level. A thesis, in this guide, refers to a more substantial piece of work, perhaps 80,000 to 100,000 words long, produced at doctoral level.

A THESIS CHAPTER

This is an obvious first choice, as the work is there already and adapting it can seem, at least initially, to be a far easier task than writing from scratch. In many cases this might be true, but there are advantages and disadvantages to this approach:

ADVANTAGES

- The material already exists in written form, so it is a safe place to start.
- You will already have crafted it beautifully, and you are proud of it.
- You can feel confidence in the conclusions you drew.

DISADVANTAGES

- You did not write the chapter for an article readership.
- You will have to recontextualise a section of the work and perhaps alter the style of writing.
- You might be too close to see how to do this, or be a little jaded with the topic.

A DRAFT CHAPTER

If you are in a position where you are working on your dissertation or thesis now, or perhaps working on a monograph, you could take advantage of this, as long as you are aware of the ramifications:

ADVANTAGES

- The work is in flux, so breaking a section of it down and working it up into an article is perhaps easier than reworking a completed and polished chapter.
- The readership of the journal can be uppermost in your mind as you work it into an article from its original, draft form.
- You will be confident in the material, and will enjoy working with it.

DISADVANTAGES

- It is very unlikely that you will be able to produce the article and then simply reinsert it back into the original piece of work: you will have to view this as a separate project.
- You might lose confidence in the organisation of the material in the original piece of work, once you have worked up an article from a draft chapter.
- As you will not have completed the original piece of work, you are laying yourself open to the chance that you would have changed your mind about some of your conclusions by its completion, which might leave you frustrated subsequently with the direction of the article which you will, by then, have submitted.

NEW RESEARCH

This moves us to the other end of the scale: the possibility of taking research which is not yet written up in any form:

ADVANTAGES

- This will be exciting, as the ideas will be fresh in your mind.
- You will not need to adapt existing writing, which can be an arduous task.
- You can focus from the outset on your target readership.

DISADVANTAGES

- This material might not have gone through the informal 'peer review' of discussion and analysis with your supervisor or mentor.
- You might feel less secure in all the facets of the material and your interpretations than in your completed work.
- You might feel, quite naturally, a little protective of material which has yet to be circulated widely.

OLD RESEARCH

Many of us have research material which we once used for purposes such as research proposals, research seminar presentations, teaching or similar. This is often in embryonic form and can be an extremely productive source of article material, but as always there are issues to consider:

ADVANTAGES

- It is pleasing to think that you are wasting nothing in your academic journey.
- As this will be in embryonic form, you can craft it into an article relatively easily.
- You will gain confidence as you write by bringing your more mature knowledge and understanding to an earlier piece of research.

DISADVANTAGES

- You may well have changed your mind about the conclusions you drew some time ago.
- Your more recent research material might diminish or even negate the relevance or validity of some aspect of the earlier research.
- You might be tempted to ignore both of these considerations and then waste your time planning and drafting what you finally realise will be a less than convincing article.

SPARE RESEARCH

This can be a delight: material about which you were enthusiastic, and which you perhaps worked up into a plan or an early draft, but which you then had to abandon because your research took a new direction. Now, it is sitting on your computer or in your notes somewhere, just begging to be turned into an article, once you have considered the pros and cons:

ADVANTAGES

- You will not have worked the material up so much that you have become bored with it.
- You will be able to disseminate an interesting idea to a wide audience.
- It might gain you feedback which could help you to develop it further in the future.

DISADVANTAGES

- Spending time on this material will take your focus away from your main area of research for a while, and might confuse your principal research direction.
- You might be tempted to try to develop it further after your article, when in fact it is a naturally end stopped area of research for you.
- Although you ostensibly abandoned it because it did not quite fit your purposes at the time, you will need to interrogate it thoroughly to ensure that it was not also flawed in some way.

JOINT RESEARCH

All joint research involves compromise. You will have decided with your research partner (or partners) both the direction of the project as it developed and the material which was to be included in the final outcome (perhaps an article, conference paper or more substantial piece of work). This can leave you brimming with ideas which were not explored at the time, or with material which was never used, so it seems like a good place to revisit for a journal article, with just a few caveats:

ADVANTAGES

- The frustration of abandoning research material can be relieved by crafting it into a journal article.
- You have a wider context into which you can place the material, as there is already some output from the joint research endeavour.
- You can feel confident that the material has already, to some extent, been scrutinised by your peers.

(Continued)

(Continued)

DISADVANTAGES

- This can be dangerous ground. You absolutely must, without fail, consult your partner researchers before you even approach this research material again.
- Your research partners may already have used some of the material, which might compromise the article you have in mind.
- If you are aiming for a single authored article, returning to this material might jeopardise that objective. You will, of course, cite both the earlier output and your fellow researchers, but you might also find it necessary to work again with your partners. This could be a fruitful process, but might frustrate you if you really wanted to work alone on an article.

RESEARCH SEMINARS

You are not always in control of which material exactly you will be working up for a research seminar. For the sake of collegiality you might well enter a research tangent and consider your research in a new light, or even conduct new research, simply in order to contribute to a research seminar. This can be a pleasure in itself, but can also bring the benefit of leaving you with material which you do not intend to use in a substantial piece of written output, but which could be used in an article:

ADVANTAGES

- The research paper you gave might be in a slightly unfinished form, with bullet pointed discussion points, for example, rather than fully worked up paragraphs. This is ideal material for the beginnings of an article.
- You will have had the benefit of immediate feedback from your peers, in what is usually an informal and productive environment, and this will give you confidence in your material and a sense of how it might develop or be edited down for an article.
- If the research is slightly away from your usual research area, you might enjoy more options in terms of journals which might take your article, rather than relying on those traditionally associated with your principal research area.

DISADVANTAGES

- When you come to review the seminar paper again, you might feel far less enthusiastic than you did at the time, because you have moved on in your thinking.
- People can be overly polite, and you might feel in retrospect that a minor comment offered quietly during the seminar actually undermines your entire hypothesis.
- If you moved away from your core research for the occasion, you might need to find new mentors for this area of research before you are happy to work it up into a finished article.

CONFERENCE PAPERS AND PRESENTATIONS

These are, without doubt, valuable sources of material for journal articles, as long as you are aware of the benefits and pitfalls:

ADVANTAGES

- A conference paper or presentation usually contains about the right amount of material for a journal article.
- You have produced it with a relatively wide audience in mind, so it should suit the relatively wide readership of a journal.
- Your tone and approach should be right: immediate and gripping whilst being intellectually sound and persuasive.

DISADVANTAGES

- You might have had your confidence in the material shattered by an unhelpful or even aggressive line of questioning at the conference. You will need to overcome this initial reaction if you are to reinterrogate the material and make a considered judgement on its value for a journal article.
- Material for a conference is often presented as a work in progress, and the conference audience will have been aware of this. Your journal article will not be the last word in this area of research, but it will need to include a greater sense of confidence and certainty about the value and interpretation of the research material.
- Giving a conference paper or presentation may have generated new partnerships and fresh ideas for joint publications or projects, and so you might want to reserve your position on publishing until you see how these prospects develop.

TEACHING MATERIAL

This source of material for a journal article is surprisingly often overlooked, perhaps because it was never intended for publication, yet it can offer interesting publication possibilities, if approached in the right way:

ADVANTAGES

- As with a conference paper or presentation, you will have tailored the material for a relatively wide audience.
- You will have received instant feedback, but from relatively non-expert audience members. The benefit of this is that they may have asked the obvious questions which a more specialised audience might overlook, but which journal readers may want answered.

(Continued)

(Continued)

- You have had to produce context as well as hypotheses, which makes it perfect for a complete journal article.

DISADVANTAGES

- If you were teaching a session at a fairly basic level, the material might not be at the right level for your chosen journal and will need to be worked up again.
- If your material was targeted towards the needs of a particular course, this might provide a poor fit for your chosen journal.
- Because the material was used in a teaching context, you might find that your article naturally tends towards a more laboured explanation than is needed for a journal readership, with the consequence that your article can seem patronising or tedious.

From anecdotal evidence, we believe that the most common piece of advice offered to researchers considering writing a journal article is simply to rework a dissertation or thesis chapter. As you may have gathered from this section, we have some reservations about this approach. It may, indeed, be the best way forward for you, and it certainly has some advantages in terms of familiarity and academic rigour and review, but it can also cause problems. Our advice is not to dismiss this approach, but also to explore every option open to you. There is no 'perfect' body of material that will transform itself effortlessly into an article, but this is not necessarily a bad thing. You will want to make the article insightful, relevant and persuasive, and work undertaken to this end must be a good thing. The decision you make now is going to be vital not only to the ultimate success of your article, but also to the ease with which you can transform research material into an elegant and persuasive piece of writing, so time spent now on considering your options will pay dividends in the future.

WHERE SHOULD YOU PLACE AN ARTICLE?

There can be a temptation to write an article and then to search around trying to find a journal whose needs seem perfectly to suit your article. This is rarely a productive way to approach the task. You will, of course, have an idea of the subject of your article, the range of material you aim to include, the argument you hope to develop and the conclusions you feel you could offer. However, by targeting your journal first, you can ensure that the way your article develops from this point on is nuanced at every stage to the needs of a clearly identified reader, and this is an important aspect of article writing.

Identifying the right journal for your work is often a challenge and there is no easy answer, but there are avenues you can pursue which will help to make the choice clear to you.

Ask your supervisor or mentor

This seems an obvious starting point, and you may have had this discussion already. A word of warning though: it is worth considering how much, and how recently, your supervisor or mentor has published. In a genuine effort to help guide you, your supervisor or mentor might point you towards a journal in which he or she has published in the past, but if this was several years ago, the journal may have changed its direction significantly since then. Similarly, there is no guarantee that your supervisor or mentor has extensive experience of publishing journal articles, and he or she may not be able to give you the most comprehensive view on the subject. The answer to this dilemma is to canvass opinion from a wide range of sources: get as much information as you reasonably can, and then make your own judgement.

Your library/resource centre

Although of course your library will not hold every journal which you might wish to target, a browse along the shelves and, more importantly, an online browse, will give you a good sense of what is out there. Be careful to avoid hunting just in your specialist area: there may well be more general journals which could offer you opportunities, so check the table of contents from back issues over several months of any that look even marginally likely to be of use to you.

Citations

Although disciplines vary in how much store they place in citations, it would be safe for you to assume that a journal which is cited regularly in scholarly output is going to be of interest to you, and this citation information is available online. As you develop your article, you will want to think in particular about a title which will have the widest possible appeal whilst still reflecting the content of the article accurately, and also your abstract, which needs to include keywords which would help other scholars find (and then cite) your article easily.

Career targets

Journals will list their editorial board or panel, both in the hard copy and online, and this might be worth checking once you have narrowed your hunt down to a few likely journals. If you would like to showcase your work in an institution other than your own, submitting an impressive article could be the way to ensure that your name, and your particular field of work, gets noticed.

Longevity

We would not want to urge you to target only the most long-lived and established of journals, as there is much to be said for targeting a new journal which more aptly covers your specialist area. The right journal for your material must be your first priority, but if you have a choice, then it makes sense to discuss with your supervisor or mentor whether a long-established or a more recently-formed journal is the best option in your particular field.

Contacts

It would be inappropriate (and probably disastrous) to approach a contact you have who happens to work on the editorial board or panel of a journal. However, if you do have a reliable contact who works for a journal in any capacity, you might want to discover anything you can about the general principles behind its decision making, such as whether it has any 'special issues' coming up, or whether it is about to branch off into a new direction.

Distribution

Whilst all journals are available globally, they will all have an initial 'home territory' where they are published, and it might be that you are unknowingly biased towards the journals published in your country of study, because you are exposed to these regularly and feel a familiarity with them. You will need to think as widely as possible about your publication. If, for example, you are living and working in America, you will have a plethora of journals to choose from, but if you have carried out research on Italian religious iconography of the sixteenth century, you will also want to consider Italian-based journals. If you are considering writing an article away from a country in which you have some experience, make contact if you can with academics in your field who are already working in that country, to ask for their advice on the most appropriate journal to approach.

Translation

Linked to the point above is the possibility of translation. Not all journals remain in simply one language, and you might want to consider the translation and distribution possibilities, if you believe your article has an especially strong international appeal.

Internet exposure

Our first word of caution here, if you are attracted to a journal which publishes in both hard copy and online, is to ensure that it has impeccable credentials, that it is peer reviewed and that it is a respected outlet. Whilst hard-copy journals also appear online for subscribers, those which are only distributed online might be perceived as having a lesser claim to academic gravitas. This will inevitably change in years to come, with the probability that many journals will only be available online, but until that time comes you need to protect yourself from any imputation of going for the potentially less esteemed option of online only publications, at least for your principal articles. This does not, of course, preclude you from publishing online occasionally – it can be an excellent way to raise awareness of your research – but you must approach this option with care (see especially Chapter 9 of this guide).

OPEN ACCESS

Whilst we have mentioned above the possibilities provided by journals which publish online as well as in hard copy, there is also another trend to consider: open access journals. The concept behind these is simple: they are intended to be free for the reader at the point of consumption, and are funded by institutions, research grants, research councils, and government bodies. These open access outlets are an excellent way for scholars to reach their readership speedily (no printing delays) and so to foster a community of scholarship. They can also be read by those in your field without the limitations of libraries having restricted funding for journals. Despite being free to access, they are not amateur productions: articles are still peer reviewed and can be of the highest standard. As with all publishing ventures you need to approach this option with your eyes open: make sure that you are working with an open access outlet which you can trust and which will further your career and promote your research appropriately. Always ensure before you go ahead that you are very clear about how publication in this online form will affect your intellectual property rights. Major journal publishers, such as SAGE, are involved in this movement, so there will be no need for you to compromise professional quality and integrity in order to gain a wide and immediate readership.

Content slant

It is not usually simply the nature of your research which will be of interest to a journal, but your treatment of that research. Journals tend to represent a particular viewpoint on a subject area, displaying an interest in certain aspects of the topics within their purview and publishing articles which fall within a particular remit. The only way to ensure that your article is the 'right' type of article for a journal is to read as many back issues as you need to explore until you get a good feel for what would be particularly appealing to that journal. This has added benefits in that you will soak up the general writing style and format which tend to be favoured by that journal, as well as some inspiration for topic areas of your own. The reason this reading research is so important is that, too often, scholars feel disappointed when their work is rejected when in reality they have produced an excellent article which is entirely worthy of publication, but they have targeted a journal whose editorial board feels that it is not a good fit with its publication agenda.

Speed of publication

This should not be a main factor in your decision making, but it is at least worth glancing at the speed at which an article is likely to progress from submission to publication. The simple answer is always 'too long', but established academics are used to this lengthy timeframe and it is unlikely to change in the near future. Although it might be a little frustrating to have to include an article on your academic CV under 'forthcoming' publications, it will not be a problem; what might be of more concern is the time it is likely to take from submission to a decision on acceptance of an article. This will not generally be a great concern to a scholar, but if you really need that publication at this stage in your career, and you need it in a hurry, it might have some bearing on your decision as you consider competing journals.

Editorial board or panel

Again, this is of secondary concern to you, but you might just check on the published output of the members of the editorial board or panel. This might give you some clues as to the possible 'slant' of a journal, although you will only be able to take this as a possible guide: it is the journal contents which will be your primary concern.

Journal presence

Certain journals will cause a 'buzz' in the academic world from time to time, as they perhaps change editorial direction or lend themselves to an emerging area of scholarly interest. Keep your ears to the ground: listen to which journals are being discussed at conferences or at your research seminars and be prepared to take the initiative and ask which journals your colleagues think are likely to be increasing their presence in the coming months. In this, do not ignore journals in a country other than the one in which you are currently working.

Specialist issues

Journals will sometimes give over an issue to a particular topic and this could be good news for you. It might be that the journal will publish papers from an academic conference, or send out a call for articles through specialist research groupings. You need to make sure that you are a member of any special interest groups in your area of work: research groupings, regular symposia, conference email lists.

Networking

Throughout this guide we will be urging you to ask for feedback on your article in various stages of its development. Your primary concern will be to gain feedback on the content, format and writing style, but you can also get a sense of how well your article might be received by journals in your area. Once you feel confident that your article is ready for submission, circulate it again asking for feedback on where you might place it. You will already have a target journal, and you will have written with this readership in mind, but being offered other possible journals once it is written gives you useful alternatives if your target journal is not as receptive as you had hoped.

Until this point your focus, naturally, has probably been on writing your article: this is the most immediate challenge you seemed to face. Now you will see that this is not so. Having a great idea for an article, and the material to support it, is an exciting moment. Planning and forming your article is also creative and satisfying. Even writing, whilst sometimes demanding, is under your control and a constructive process, but it is placing your article which is likely to be your greatest challenge. Spending time and energy researching journals and finding the perfect outlet for your work is not time wasted: it is an essential part of the process and one which you cannot afford to neglect. Finding the best journal at the best time will save you hours of wasted time and energy later, and will help hugely in the task we come to next: selecting a topic and adapting your work.

YOUR ARTICLE AND YOUR ACADEMIC STANDING

We have already asked you to consider, in brief, how the publication of an article might have a positive impact on your career, if you are working within academia. Here we want to consider two aspects of this in detail: impact and the REF (Research Excellence Framework), which has replaced the RAE (Research Assessment Exercise) in the UK. Similar organisations exist throughout the world, so the advice we are offering here will be of relevance to you wherever you are carrying out your research and publishing your results.

These two factors, impact and the REF, will undoubtedly have a bearing on your published output and you ignore them at your peril. It is no longer enough simply to publish what you like, where you like, and assume that this will be career enhancing in and of itself. Indeed, one could argue that this never was truly the case.

We would not suggest that you need to be constrained in all the plans you are making by either impact or the REF – that would make no sense either intellectually or practically; what we are suggesting is that you recognise and understand the effect these aspects of academic life will have on your published output. Unfortunately it is not possible in a guide of this length to explore and delineate every ramification of them (although a further book in this series will offer you this detail). What we can give you is a broad guide to how things work, a 'heads up' on how and when you should take them into consideration.

Let's look at 'impact' first. The inverted commas around that term are deliberate, indicative of both the importance this word has acquired in recent times and the complexity of interpreting it within the context of the REF. The idea itself is relatively simple: academic research output will be judged (and therefore, through the REF, funds will be allocated) in part by the impact it can be proved to have. In short, this means that, wherever possible, the research presented in a journal article, and the way that it is presented, must be shown to have an effect (cultural, economical, intellectual or educational) both within and beyond academia.

In some areas, this was always a reasonably easy task, as research led naturally to a benefit for the economy or could be shown, with little effort, to have an impact beyond the walls of higher education institutions. In other areas it is very much more difficult, but it still must be addressed. For the foreseeable future, it would just not make sense to ignore it.

If you are coming to the idea of impact anew, you might find it daunting, so here are some guidelines to help you:

1 Rather than 'bolting on' the idea of impact once you have written the article, consider it in the early planning stages. This does not necessarily mean altering the content, but it might mean highlighting certain aspects of your research over others.

2 Consider impact in terms of *where* you publish. An article which you originally intended for a small, select publication might well have more impact if you were to consider submitting it to a different journal.

3 Think of your audience. No journal article is set in stone. You may be able to launch from one article to another, the second focusing on one aspect of your research which you feel sure will deliver more impact.

4 Understand the impact framework of your department. The research leaders in your department will be creating a research narrative for the REF, and impact will be part of that narrative. By working in conjunction with colleagues you may well find that your research fits nicely within a wider research grouping, which is being used to prove impact for your department's research output.

5 Seek advice. You will not be expected to work through this challenge on your own. There will be experts in your institution who will have studied the requirement documentation for impact carefully, and will be able to guide you in this area, so forget the idea of working in isolation to produce your perfect article: seek advice early and often.

6 Try not to panic. If you are not working in an area where impact is obvious (that is, your research is likely to produce patentable ideas, or have a direct impact on the world around you), you might be tempted to throw your hands up in despair, or to simply assume that nothing you have done so far is worth pursuing. This is not going to be the case. You will not need to abandon your plans for an article, nor will you need to produce something radically different from your first intentions. You simply need to factor impact into your thinking about the article.

7 Stay positive. As scholars we are all enthusiastic about our research, but the imposition of impact as a criterion can too easily lead us to assume that we just cannot compete, cannot produce anything from our research which is relevant to the need for impact. This leads, understandably, to a negative view of the process (which is just about bearable) but also, potentially, to us feeling negative about our research (and this certainly is not to be tolerated). You are dedicating years of your life to your research, so it must be important to you. All that the impact requirement is doing is asking you to reveal its importance to others and to show, where you can, that it is of benefit to the wider community. If you see this as a positive challenge it will make the whole process easier.

8 Be open to sharing. You may be used to disseminating your research in a narrow field of experts, and there is great pleasure to be gained from this. You are communicating with like minded individuals and enjoying the

challenges and benefits that this brings. However, this does not mean that you should be exclusive in your approach. Considering other outlets for your research, as we will suggest several times in this guide, can also bring benefits, as you see your work being considered more widely and having an impact on those who may not be in the tight circle of experts, but who will nevertheless benefit from the work you have done.

The REF is an integral part of lives as scholars, and it must become an embedded feature of your planning; this can be to your advantage. The process by which research output is judged in this way allows you to consider your work in the context of the wider world of academia, and to boost your career as a direct result of your publications. Periodically, your department will be judged on its publication performance (amongst other things, such as the vitality of the research environment) and you will naturally want to be part of this process. You will want to ensure that your publications are 'returned' as part of the REF submission, so you will want to do your best to ensure that you put the best face of your research forward.

If you were regularly producing excellent articles in leading journals in your area, along with a monograph and some chapters in prestigious publications, you could assume that you would be lauded within both your department and the REF process. However, for most of us it is more a case of being selective and using our time wisely to create output which will be of most benefit to our careers at every stage.

The REF makes judgements about the *quality* of your research and this is important. Although one would expect to see high quality research in a leading journal, this does not mean that it does not exist, in abundance, elsewhere. This means that, from your perspective, you should not assume that only a leading journal will do. Given the level of submissions to leading journals, and the inevitable level of rejection just because of the sheer volume of submissions, it is worth seeking advice on the strategic placement of your article.

Judgements are made by REF panels, and each panel might take a slightly different view of how to assess research excellence, albeit within the overarching guidelines of the process. With this in mind, it makes sense for you to talk to the research leaders and managers in your department to get a better idea of the view they are taking as to what will be most beneficial in terms of your department's submission.

The REF requires you to submit 'outputs', it does not specify that each output must be a huge monograph which is going to be the leading text in its field for years to come. It would be pleasing to produce this, of course, but again you must be canny with your time and effort and seek advice on which type of publication best suits the current position of your research and the other demands upon your academic life.

You will notice that in this discussion of impact and the REF we have urged you repeatedly to seek the advice of others, and this is perhaps the most important guidance we can offer. Every single academic institution and department, throughout the world, will take a view on this, based upon the strengths of the department and the variety of research being carried out within it. This is to your benefit: use the expertise around you to help craft the best possible journal article not just in terms of your research, but also in a way that produces maximum impact: not only the impact defined by the REF, but also the impact on academia that you want to make in your career.

USEFUL WEBSITES

Open access opportunities

www.uk.sagepub.com/sageopen.sp
www.eprints.org/openaccess

Web of Knowledge (citation and journal database)

http://wok.mimas.ac.uk

Higher Education Funding Council for England

www.hefce.ac.uk/research/ref/

Research Councils' Websites

www.rcuk.ac.uk
www.ahrc.ac.uk
www.esrc.ac.uk
www.epsrc.ac.uk
www.bbsrc.ac.uk
www.mrc.ac.uk
www.nerc.ac.uk
www.stfc.ac.uk

Researcher Development Framework

www.vitae.ac.uk/policy-practice/234301/Researcher-Development-Framework.html

2

SELECTING YOUR TOPIC/ ADAPTING YOUR WORK

CHAPTER OVERVIEW

This chapter will be especially helpful if:

- Some of your research material could be crafted into an article, but you are struggling to see it in this context.
- An area of your research output which could produce an article has already been reworked several times and you are simply bored with it.
- You have little or no experience in adapting material.
- You cannot seem to find quite the right material for an article.
- You tend to struggle in bringing your research material under control.

SELECTING YOUR TOPIC

The topic you choose for an article is clearly up to you, but we would like to offer you some brief points to guide you:

Enjoy the process

If you have been struck with an interesting idea for an article, give yourself the time and space to work out whether it will work as a journal article, or might be better used elsewhere. Planning an outline of the article will give you a sense of whether the idea holds up and can be developed into an article. This is a hugely creative part of the process, so there is no need to think that you are simply indulging in mental doodling: this could be your perfect article.

Trust your instinct

There is nothing like mentioning the idea of an article to invite a plethora of well-meaning advice. However much you respect those who are seeking to help you, this is *your* article. If you feel, having given it sufficient consideration, that a topic is not going to deliver the type of article you want to produce at this stage of your career and for your chosen journal, it is essential that you look elsewhere for a more suitable topic.

Consider your source material

The boxes in Chapter 1 will have given you a clearer idea of the advantages and disadvantages of working up an article from different sources. You know how you work best, so if any of the disadvantages outlined there have put you off a particular approach, it might be best, at least for now, to avoid the topic area which you have covered in that potential source material. We are considering in this chapter the notion of you selecting and adapting *your* work, and this is important. Whilst it is always fascinating to see how your research arose and to be able to survey the work already carried out in your area, an article cannot simply be a sophisticated literature review. You must do more than simply survey what is there already: your article must show your work in context, of course, but it must be an original piece of work based upon your research. That is what is going to interest editorial panels and readers alike and will form the basis of a successful submission.

Research the market

We cannot stress this enough. The most proficient article in the academic world will go nowhere if it is presented to a journal for which it is not suited. You will need to carry out thorough research on your target journals in order to see which topic, of the several available to you, would be most appealing to your chosen journal.

Narrow your topic

You would be an unusual scholar if you have not already been faced with the need to narrow down your topic of research in order to produce an effective output. This is the constant challenge faced by all academics. We have ideas all of the time (it is in our nature), yet we must focus, always reducing the number of research questions until the material which results from those questions fits neatly into the amount of time and space we have available to disseminate our research. The phrase 'research questions' is important here. It is quite difficult, and demoralising, to try to edit a finished article to half its original size, and the resulting article is usually far less effective than if you had narrowed down your research questions far earlier in process. It is for this reason, amongst others, that productive planning becomes so important to writers of journal articles.

Test your confidence

We are happy to keep repeating, as often as you can bear to hear it, that no article can ever represent the last word on any topic area. It would be a boring and rather redundant academic world if it could. However, you need to feel that your article not only represents an interesting and, perhaps, challenging viewpoint, but also that it is based upon hypotheses in which you can feel confident and which are supported by rigorous and reliable research. You will obviously feel confident about this at the outset, otherwise you would not be contemplating writing an article, but you will need to be brave here. Keep assessing your level of confidence at every stage of the process, from the planning, to the draft article, to the revisions and on to the final product. There is always a strong temptation to keep going once you have dedicated hard work and precious time to the early stages of the process, but remember that if you do abandon that topic area for a while and try out another for an article, the work is not wasted: you are simply reserving that material for the future.

ADAPTING YOUR WORK

Planning, forwards and backwards

In Chapter 3 we will be discussing different planning methods, and each of these relies on you being able to take a step back from your material in order to organise it effectively. If you are starting from raw material, shaping new research data which has not been used elsewhere, the process is relatively straightforward. You will be planning forward, and the plan will be forming as the article takes shape in your mind. If, as might well be the case, you are

producing your article from material which has already been written up elsewhere, the procedure can feel more artificial and at times a little awkward. In
this case you will be planning backwards. The material has already been formed
into a piece of written work, or a document for a seminar or teaching session,
and your task is to deconstruct and reconstruct it so as to make it work for a
journal article.

If you are working from raw material, you might simply want to skim read
this next section and then focus on Chapter 3. If you are reusing or reworking
material which has already taken shape in some form, we would like to work
with you through an overview of the ways in which you might be using plans
to manoeuvre material into a new shape. You will have one (or more) of several
objectives:

- reusing material;
- reducing material;
- reinforcing an argument;
- reinventing your perspective;
- ruling your material.

Reusing material

As we have already suggested, it would be exceptional, perhaps impossible, to
find any piece of writing you have produced which would fit exactly into an
article for publication. A journal article will have, generally, a well defined
readership and it is to these readers that you must write. So, you will be targeting your article to suit their needs. Material you have used for teaching is likely
to contain some material which is too general or basic in nature, material
contained within a thesis or dissertation chapter will be reliant upon discussions you have had elsewhere in the work, and the readers of the journal will
not have the benefit of these discussions. Most importantly, your focus as a
writer, the image you want to present, will differ between this type of writing
and an article. For much of the writing you produce for assessment of one kind
or another you are effectively saying 'Look how much I know about this! Look
at how well I can use the material I have found!' As the writer of a journal
article, your readers will assume that you have mastered this area of your subject, and your writing will support this belief, but their interest is in how well
you use your knowledge and material to create an argument which is engaging, perhaps contentious, and certainly adding something to the discussions
within your chosen field of expertise.

In Chapter 1 we talked about the different options you have in terms of
reusing material of various kinds: here we want to focus on the use of planning
as a means to do this. If you are going to reuse material for an article, the first
thing you need to do is to unpick the original piece of writing. Simply cutting

and pasting whole sentences or paragraphs is usually a recipe for disaster, because you are trying to fit writing into a setting for which it was never intended. Instead, you will want to work through your original piece of writing and retrospectively plan it, using one of the planning methods we demonstrate in Chapter 3. Once you have this plan, you will be able to make decisions about what to exclude from your original piece, if anything, and what you might need to add to make it work as an article.

Reducing material

Having asserted that cutting and pasting existing writing is rarely conducive to producing an impressive article, we should offer a similar warning with regard to editing out material from an existing piece of writing and hoping to make it hang together as a fluent and persuasive article. This is not only extremely difficult to do effectively, it is also hugely time consuming; for most writers it is quicker and more effective to go back to the planning stage. In this way you can delete whole sections of the plan and see at a glance whether the material you have left will work cohesively as an article.

It is unnervingly difficult to take this type of overview once you have reduced a piece of writing just by deleting sections, paragraphs and sentences, as you will inevitably 'ghost in' many of the words which, in reality, you have just removed. It also has a distressingly detrimental effect on your writing style. Although you may not make the mistake of explicitly referring to material which is no longer part of your reduced article, you are likely to write on the assumption that the readers know more than you have given them, as your writing will tend to be nuanced towards the background of a much longer piece of writing. You need to alienate yourself from the original writing in order to avoid this effect, and planning is one way to do this.

Reinforcing an argument

Any piece of writing you have produced will be seeking to persuade your reader of something, and this point is often overlooked if you simply try to reword an existing piece of writing in order to shape it into an article. Without necessarily any conscious effort on your part, your writing style will have reinforced your argument, yet you will probably be aiming to persuade a journal readership of something slightly different. Your material will all be there in your original piece of writing, and will still be valid, but the way in which you present that material will differ depending upon the point you are trying to make. Simply reusing sections of writing and trying to surround them with a winning argument is unlikely to work: going back to the bare bones of your research and building an argument will be more effective. Once you have identified the salient points for your article, you will be in a position to judge whether you need to reorder those points, or remove some of them, or perhaps add additional material in order to create the most effective argument in the context within which you are writing.

Reinventing your perspective

It is always necessary to consider your reader when you are writing, and this is a fairly simple and instinctive stance to take for most of us, most of the time. However, if you are taking some writing produced for one type of reader (a teaching group, for example, or external examiners in a viva) and trying to target it to another type of reader (in this case, the reader of a particular journal) you are likely to miss your mark unless you reconsider your perspective. It is, of course, possible to simply cut and paste your original piece of writing and then string it all together in a new format, but once you ask a colleague or mentor to read it, you might be disappointed in the response. What seems to you to be clear (after all, you wrote the original piece) may well be entirely unclear to a new readership. Again, we would advise a stripping back and reworking as the best way to avoid this disheartening result.

Ruling your material

Mastering your research is a vital element in becoming a successful researcher, and the process of reusing material is the one that, over the years, we have seen causing problems for even relatively experienced researchers. It happens like this. You have a word count for your article, and an existing piece of writing which you think will suit a journal very well. You are aware that the original piece is twice as long as the word count of the article but, undaunted, you begin to cut down the writing by deleting and cutting and pasting. As you go along, you occasionally find that, by deleting a section, you will have to add a few words of explanation to the remaining material in order to contextualise it. Then you find that you have to add a substantial opening section in order to focus on the interests of the journal readership. You are loath to take out too much of the research data because the readers might find it useful (and, if you are honest with yourself, you spent ages bringing it together in the first place and would like the world to admire it). Before you realise what is happening, you have a new piece of writing, well sculpted into a journal article, which focuses on your new argument and the journal readership – and it is precisely as long as the original piece of writing. You may have done well to reinvent the piece, but you have entirely failed to rule your material. Again, stepping back and reworking the material in the planning phase will eliminate this problem entirely, as long as you are ruthless enough.

Being ruthless and gaining a new perspective just seems to come easily to some researchers. They are able to take a lengthy piece of writing, or a substantial amount of teaching material, and simply see their way through to the heart of what they want to include in a journal article. For most of us, it is not nearly that easy. If you find that you tend to get bogged down in the detail and that you struggle to find your way through to a new plan, there are techniques you might use to help.

In Chapter 3 we will go into detail about the differing planning methods open to you and the various ways in which you might use them. Here we will be using a brainstorm and a very basic spider chart. If you are completely unfamiliar with these planning methods you might want to read sections of Chapter 3 now.

Use your memory

This is the most direct way to move from a piece of writing to a retrospective plan. Rather than going back to a piece of writing and beginning to work through it, try to remember what is was that you produced. Avoid the temptation to take even the tiniest peek at the writing itself, but instead force yourself to remember. You can usefully begin with a brainstorm, then move on to a more organised plan, considering at each stage whether you are capturing too much, or too little, of the relevant information. The theory behind this technique is that you are more likely to take an objective overview of what you were trying to say if you remove yourself from the detail of the text in this way. This is easier to grasp if you see it in practice.

Imagine for a moment that one of the authors of this guide has chosen to take a section from a chapter of her (fictional) thesis, entitled 'Childbirth through the ages', and wants to turn it into the basis of a journal article with a different slant, entitled 'The case for home births in a time of economic recession'. You can see instantly from these titles that the pieces of writing are aimed at different readerships and so will need to differ in style, in word count, in the selection of material and in the way in which it is ordered. Nevertheless, the original piece of writing from her thesis, shown below, could be a valid starting point for the article:

> The business of midwifery has long been contentious. As was shown in Chapter 1 of this thesis, as long ago as the Early Modern period the birthing chamber was the scene of sharp divisions, between the female carers and 'wise women' who would help the mother in an amateur way, the female midwives and the increasingly present 'man midwives', and between all of these figures and the physicians and surgeons. Subsequent chapters have demonstrated that this contention has remained, to a greater or lesser degree, and divisions still exist today.

The most noticeable of these is perhaps the choices women make not just about who is present at the birth, and who will tend to their needs, but also about where that birth will take place. The Howe Study of 2002 (see Appendix J) focused on six aspects of this topic:

- the historic precedents for hospital and home births;
- the social pressure for either hospital or home births;
- the satisfaction of the mother in the care she receives in labour;
- the views of midwives and physicians;
- the management of labour wards;
- the relative outcomes in terms of infant health.

Howe was able to prove an increased satisfaction expressed by those women in his study who were given a choice between home and hospital births, and this research also pointed to a socio-economic benefit to offering home birth options.

In 2006, the case of *Hillier vs Greenfelt* (see Chapter 6, p. 101) revealed the lengths to which women would go to remain in their own homes, with the right level of midwifery care, throughout all stages of labour. In contrast, *James vs Easthill Primary Care Trust* (2007) outlines for us the arguments raised by some medical practitioners against too great a swing towards home births as the norm, principally citing the safety of mother and child but recognising the cost benefits of home births to which the judge in *Hillier vs Greenfelt* alluded.

Recent studies in Sweden seem to make a convincing case for home births as the norm, with hospitalisation only to be considered in specific circumstances, and these studies will be explored in more detail in the following chapter. For the purposes of my argument here, the recent work by Lazurro, and the Italian experience he captured in his study *Women and Children First* (2010), is more pertinent. In Lazurro's fascinating study he looks at rates of postnatal depression, going back to the 1960s, and claims that hospital births, especially in rural areas, show a sustained link with higher rates of postnatal depression.

He goes on to argue that whilst hospital births can provide initial cost benefits, the cost of caring for mothers with severe postnatal depression can be shown to outweigh this benefit. His primary focus is on the subsequent development of the children of these mothers, asserting that society pays too high a price for insisting upon hospital births as the norm. However, he is not advocating home births as the default position within society, but rather argues that choice is what matters. Those women who were given the choice as to where to give birth, and who was to attend the birth, clearly showed greater satisfaction with the process and decreased incidence of postnatal depression. Lazurro cautions that this cannot be the only, or even necessarily the primary, cause for postnatal depression amongst so many variables, but his work does challenge us to look again at this aspect of childbirth. It seems that we might not have moved as far from the Early Modern birthing chamber as we might have assumed: the tensions still exist, the contentions are still there; we might have ejected the 'wise women' of that era, but we now need to find a new and wiser way to move forward as a society.

The first thing the writer will do is to take a large piece of paper and a thick pen and brainstorm what she remembers. The big paper and pen are significant here, by the way, as they will remind her that she is trying to remember the big, bold ideas in the original, rather than allowing herself to be distracted by too much detail. She will hope, in fact, that she has forgotten much of the detail by now and that only the most salient points will have been left in her memory.

Her initial brainstorm might look like this:

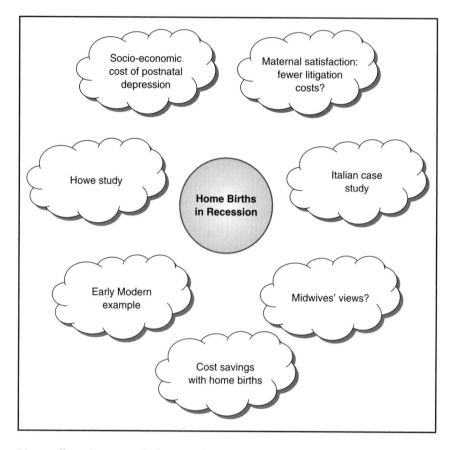

You will notice several things when you look at this brainstorm. She has picked out the key points as she remembered them, and these will be more or less useful to her as she progresses:

- She picked up the Early Modern example, which, perhaps, was inevitable given that it opened the piece. It was highly relevant in the context of her thesis as a whole, so as to tie it all together, but is less so here. Nevertheless, she does quite like the opening and ending of the extract so she might like to reuse them if she has space.
- The Howe Study is on here, but without the detail of the original. In the extract, the use of bullet points and the graph which she had included in an appendix might tend to obscure her ability to take an overview of the piece as a whole, and so she will be pleased to have avoided this pitfall by refusing to look back at the original before carrying out this brainstorm. She will not

want to cover the Howe Study in detail here, but can pick out the bullet points which she judges to be most relevant.

- She has forgotten to include the court cases, but she has remembered that somewhere she mentioned the cost savings that might be achieved through home births. Later on, she will be able to cite the relevant cases in her article.
- It is not surprising that she forgot the example of Sweden. It was mentioned only in passing, and was to be referred to in more detail in a later chapter. She may consider including it later, but it is not yet obviously relevant.
- The Italian case study did stick in her mind, so much so that she effectively included it twice in her brainstorm: both under 'Italian case study' and 'Socio-economic cost of postnatal depression'. Not only was this a vivid part of the original piece, she now intends to make it the mainstay of her new article.
- She has also included two notes which are not explicitly included in the original piece of writing: the views of midwives and possible cost of litigation related to restricted maternal choice. The first of these is hardly mentioned at all, but could be relevant to her article (it is intended for a journal with a large readership amongst midwives) and the latter is perhaps implied but might need to be discussed in more detail in her article. On the other hand, she may decide that litigation is not relevant to her argument as it develops in her later planning stages, in which case she will abandon this point.

Already we can see that the article which is emerging will be different from the original. The slant of the argument has changed, the focus tightened, and the potential word count reduced. Another key benefit of this technique is that the writer has ended up with six key points, and the Early Modern example which will not be a point in itself, but might provide an introduction and/or conclusion to the article. This is about the right number of main areas for the article; if she had allowed herself to refer back to the original before brain-storming she would have been swamped with many more points and would then have struggled to control the material.

How well this technique will work depends on three things: the age of the original piece of work, the strength of your memory and the type of memory you have. Obviously you are likely to remember fewer points if you produced the original piece of writing some time ago; conversely, for a more recent piece of writing you might find that you are remembering far too many points. If you have a good memory you will remember far more than if your memory is generally poor. You will also be affected by the type of memory function you have. For those who take in written information easily, this example would work well; for those who have an aural memory, they are more likely to remember points from teaching materials or conference papers which they have delivered out loud.

Before we look at how the writer might develop this example beyond the initial brainstorm, we need to consider how you might overcome these poten-tial hurdles. If you remember far too much, and so struggle to pick out the salient points even after some time, you might try this approach.

Use a friend

For some of us, writing points down can be a problem. Our memories are excellent and so, given this exercise, we would be able to replicate the original piece of writing almost word for word, and our brainstorm would be of little use as all of the points made in the original article would appear there. If this is the case for you, one way to eliminate the problem is to avoid writing anything down before you have mediated it through speech. Ask a fellow researcher, a friend or your mentor or supervisor (and, ideally, several of them at the same time) to sit with you while you explain the outline of the original text and then transcribe it into a brainstorm. Ask them to be firm with you, pulling you up whenever you seem to be giving them too much detail, and constantly reminding you of the readership and purpose of your intended article. Allow them to ask questions: they will often ask the very obvious questions which you have failed to address in your eagerness to capture the detail. Once you have produced the brainstorm, ask them to help you to narrow it down so that you delete irrelevant points at this very early stage.

You might be the sort of researcher who has the opposite problem, struggling to remember anything very much at all, or remembering some random points but losing the overall shape of the piece. If this seems to be the case for you, it is worth taking a different approach.

Use a highlighter

You will want to distinguish between your original piece and the article you are planning, but you know that you are not going to be able to recall enough to make a brainstorm work simply from memory. Take the initial piece of writing and use a highlighter pen to pick out the most important points, forcing yourself to highlight only those points which seem relevant to the new article, and trying to avoid picking out all of the detailed information: just because it is detailed data does not mean that it is relevant to your current purpose. If you find yourself, at the end of the exercise, with a piece of text fairly much covered in highlighter you will know that things have gone wrong. Print out a new copy of the text and start again, being ruthless in your drive to eliminate any extraneous points. Again, having someone alongside you to query why you are highlighting certain points can be useful as you train yourself to be more selective.

It still makes sense to produce a brainstorm once you have finished with the highlighter pen. If you try to produce a more detailed plan straight from the highlighted text you will constantly be tempted to include details which are unnecessary to your purpose. Creating a brainstorm also gives you the chance to narrow down your focus even further by requiring you to examine, yet again, your highlighted points and consider whether to include them.

Once you have a completed brainstorm, however you have arrived at it, you will be ready to move on to the next stage of the process of adaptation: producing a more detailed plan. The examples in Chapter 3 will show you how a variety of subject areas can be worked through different planning methods; here we will use a spider chart to show how this example might have developed from the brainstorm we produced.

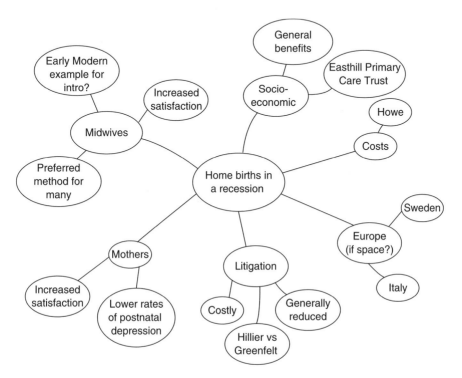

FIGURE 1

You will see that the plan has changed yet again in the move across from a brainstorm of initial ideas into the more formal structure of a spider chart. Some things have been abandoned, whilst others have been included and expanded. Most importantly, the writer now has a good idea of the likely shape of her article, because the spider chart has allowed her to show not only the most important points to include, but also those points which are secondary: these are the points which are most likely to be abandoned if the article threatens to become much too long.

The length of the article is the next issue she will consider. She will have an approximate idea of how many words might be needed for each section of the plan and so will be able to make a judgement now as to whether any sections can be abandoned without harming the article overall. It is far easier to lop off a section of the plan at this stage than to write and rewrite the article in the future. This is where the writer could rely on the experience of others, and it is a good time to take the spider chart to colleagues to discuss whether they think the argument hangs together as it is planned, and whether, in their view, it is likely to be too long or too short. Any points which are abandoned now can, of course, be picked up later from the plan if the word count allows.

For some writers, a spider chart is enough. They can happily write an article from this type of plan and would rather not plan in more detail. For many of us, however, it is a good idea to transfer the spider chart into a bullet pointed list plan. In doing this, you will see the proposed order of information set out clearly, as it will appear in the article, and this allows you to make last minute changes before you write. If you are going to be writing an article which contains a large proportion of technical information, it allows you to include this now, in your list plan, so that you can feel confident that nothing will be omitted once you are writing.

For the example we have given here, the list plan could look like this:

THE CASE FOR HOME BIRTHS IN A TIME OF ECONOMIC RECESSION

INTRODUCTION

The case of Early Modern midwives, leading into first section.

MIDWIVES

Home births are often the preferred method of delivery for midwives.
Some find increased job satisfaction with home births.

MOTHERS

Studies show increased maternal satisfaction with home birth system.
Lower rates of postnatal depression.

LITIGATION

Some mothers have gone to great lengths to have a home birth.
Litigation is costly and should be avoided where possible.
Home birth system tends to reduce the rate of litigation.

COSTS

Exploration of section of Howe study on cost benefits.

SOCIO-ECONOMIC

Link also to Howe study above – but remember *James vs Easthill Primary Care Trust* for balance and argument against socio-economic benefits.

EUROPE

If there is space enough, look at Italy and Sweden. If there is not enough space to do a full section on this, maybe mention them in passing in the other sections.

CONCLUSION

This issue will continue to be contentious, but there are good reasons to consider a greater adoption of the home birthing system in the UK.

Notice that this list plan still feels quite flexible. It is written in a note-like form, with a sense that the writer is still deciding exactly what to include, depending on how the argument develops and the word count fills out. This is as it should be: it will help you to avoid being too stilted in your writing and it allows you to gain full control as you write, rather than imposing it artificially in the planning stages.

A list plan also allows you to do something else – but only with great caution. The dangers of simply cutting and pasting from an existing piece of work still exist, but at this stage you could risk cutting and pasting a sentence here and there, if you felt that you expressed yourself exceptionally well in the original piece and could not better it now. In practice, by this stage most scholars prefer simply to begin writing again from a blank page, but you do at least have the option of cutting and pasting a little if you feel this would help you. You will need to be very selective about it, but it could give you a confidence boost and get you into the right frame of mind before you begin to write.

It would be logical to assume that now we are going to urge you to start writing, having done so much preparation, but there is one more thing you need to do before you begin to write:

Give yourself time

Leave time to ponder. Make a first draft plan of the points based upon your reworking of the original piece of writing, using the techniques highlighted here, then leave it to one side for a while, ideally for several days. Then, come back to the plan and make a judgement on whether or not you can reduce it to sharpen up your focus and strengthen your argument. Alternatively, you might feel that it is thin in some places and so needs a little more material to maintain its force. It may take you several attempts, but you will get to the point where the plan rests easily in a way that you feel would work well. When you start to feel a genuine urge to begin writing (rather than simply responding to the external pressure to write) you will be at the right stage.

3

PLANNING AND GETTING STARTED

CHAPTER OVERVIEW

This chapter will be especially helpful if:

- You have tended not to plan your written output in the past.
- You do not feel confident about how to plan your article.
- You want to save yourself time at the writing stage.
- You are not sure which planning method would suit either your material or the way that your brain works.
- You think planning is the 'boring' bit of writing (it is not, so read on!)

Planning your article is going to be essential. As you will gather from the previous chapter, we are aware that you might be writing from scratch, or you might be revising and reworking material which you have written up in some form before. The planning methods discussed here will work for both approaches, either to help you to gather together and organise new material, or to analyse, strip back and reform older material.

It is always a sensible idea to plan your written output, in greater or lesser detail dependent upon the finished product, but a plan for an article serves more functions than you might expect. As well as the most obvious function, that of organising your material, a plan can also:

- Be used as a discussion document.
- Nuance your writing style.
- Speed the production process.

- Control the word count.
- Increase the impact of your article.

We will look later in this chapter at the ways in which you might use a plan to organise your material, but here we will consider in more detail these additional benefits.

A discussion document

Throughout the stages of producing your article you are likely to be discussing it with various people, from your supervisor or mentor, to fellow researchers, to other colleagues with whom you work. In the early stages these conversations will be rather vague, with perhaps no more than the kernel of an idea under discussion, and this is as it should be. What you are asking for is a general impression of whether your colleagues feel that your idea will make a good article, and perhaps you will be asking for some suggestions as to where you might try to place it.

As the process moves on, you will naturally be refining your ideas and starting to create an argument which will run through your article, and at this stage general or unfocused conversations can be a danger. People will naturally want to help you and so will make suggestions of their own as to what you might include, and will put forward their own ideas as to how your argument could develop. Almost before you realise this is happening, your compact and incisive idea for an article will have become a dissertation in prospect, and you could have lost your way entirely. This is where a good plan comes in. If, in these later discussions, you can show your colleagues a detailed plan of how you think the article might develop, you will be able to instigate far more focused discussions, which will enhance the development of your article rather than muddying the waters.

When you are using a plan to develop your article, try always to discuss it with others when you have plenty of time to do so (a hurried conversation with your supervisor in a corridor, for example, is never a good idea) and have pen and paper ready. This will help to keep the focus on your original plan, and will also allow you to jot down any new ideas which arise from it. It is often the case, as in most research activity, that one idea spawns another, and connections are made in discussions which you would not have seen alone. Under ideal circumstances, the discussions surrounding your plan will provide ideas for several future articles.

Your writing style

Although we would not argue that working up a plan for an article will have a huge effect on your writing style, it can make some difference, and this might be all that you need. If you have been producing lengthy, complex chapters for a dissertation or thesis, you will want to encourage in yourself a more succinct style of writing. On the other hand, if you have been teaching recently and working from a series of bullet pointed lists on handouts or a data projector, you will want your style to become a little more fluid and expansive for your article. Using particular planning methods can help to settle your mind into taking the right approach to this next writing task. As we go through different planning methods with you, we will be making mention of how they might affect your writing style.

Speeding up the process

We will be discussing, in Chapter 4, the particular problem of writer's block and we consider there how a plan might help you through that process. However, the usefulness of a plan to speed the process of writing is not restricted just to those suffering from that frustrating condition. A plan can help all of us to write more fluently and to greater effect.

One of the most common objections amongst research students when it is suggested that they make a detailed plan for a project is that it will be too time consuming and cumbersome. Surely, they ask, it is easier and quicker just to get on and write something? In reality, this is rarely the case. Writing an unplanned article leaves you with a first draft that is probably some considerable distance from the finished product, and you then waste hours of your time cutting and pasting, changing your mind, fiddling and checking, until you reach the finished article, all of which is both time consuming and demoralising. In addition to this, your finished article is likely to be less polished than you had hoped. We are none of us terribly good at thinking and writing at the same time: we need to use a plan to think through the problems that are likely to arise in our argument and to organise our material in the best way possible. Once this has been achieved, we can write an article far more quickly and, as importantly, we will have the mental space to consider just how to express ourselves in the best way possible. Learning to plan effectively is one of the best kept secrets of most successful academics.

Controlling the word count

A strict word count, such as you are likely to have for a journal article, can have a deadening effect on the writing process. If part of your mind is constantly worrying about the word count, you might find it difficult to focus sufficiently on the task ahead of you. Additionally, if you become concerned as you write that you might exceed the word count, sections of your article may become 'squashed' as you write. That is, your writing will become almost note-like, a point will be made only sketchily before you move on to the next, and the conclusions you are drawing will seem hasty and tentative rather than confident and forceful.

It is for this reason that we would always urge writers to try to forget the word count as much as possible when they are actually in the process of writing. It is generally far better simply to write and get the article down in draft form and then go back to edit it to the right length. Of course, as we mentioned earlier in this chapter, if you have no plan this can lead to disaster, but if you have a detailed plan, this strategy should work well, as long as your plan is realistic, and that is the key to success with word counts.

In the past you will have produced essays, papers and perhaps far lengthier pieces of writing, and if you are used to planning you will have a good sense of how a plan should 'look and feel' if it is to produce an article of the right length. If you have not planned much in the past, you might be far less certain of how your plan should look before you begin to write.

There are several ways you might gain some certainty:

- You could ask your supervisor or mentor, or any other colleague experienced in producing articles, to look at your plan with a view simply to considering how well it will work according to the word count.
- You could look back at a piece of writing you have produced of a similar word count, and retrospectively plan it, taking the salient points from the piece and ordering them according to one or other of the planning methods we will be discussing in this chapter.
- You might choose to produce your plan as a presentation and try giving the presentation, equating a certain amount of time speaking aloud to a certain number of words, to ensure that you have the right amount of material.

We talk about all of these approaches in this guide, so you can decide on the best method for you, but here we want to stress the importance of this relation between plan and word count. It is time consuming and frustrating to keep removing sections from an article once you realise that you have seriously exceeded the stipulated word count. A little light editing can be an enjoyable, creative activity; wholesale slashing is not. Added to this, your finished article after the slashing will show the scars of what you have had to do. So, you use your plan to reduce the article before you even start to write. It is relatively easy to lop off whole sections of a plan, and of course these can be put aside for use in future articles, and once you have a plan which you feel fairly sure will fit your word count, you will write with greater enthusiasm and confidence.

Increasing impact

You will, naturally, want to write in the most persuasive and impressive style possible for your article and this guide will help you to do that, but the first part of this endeavour does not lie with writing, but with planning. As a researcher you can often indulge in quite a diffuse style of writing, in some cases because this is what is required. You are taking your reader through a mass of material in order to underpin your initial hypothesis and, later, you will be analysing the material and testing the hypothesis, all the time taking your reader along with you. In an article you inevitably have to make some – although not too many – assumptions, about the level of knowledge of the likely readers, of their understanding of your initial hypothesis and of their ability to follow you at some speed. A lengthy exposition of your hypothesis would be inappropriate, as would a laborious trip through all of your material. Instead, you are being asked to get to the point at reasonable speed and to make the most of the space you have available in order to create the greatest impact. Planning helps you to do this. You can make early decisions about what to discard and what to retain in order to support your argument and so make your article as incisive and engaging as possible.

Competing planning methods

We refer here to 'competing' methods because each planning method has advantages and potential disadvantages, depending on what you are trying to achieve by using it. You will need to discover which methods suit you best – if you use a method which does not work in the same way your brain works, you could confuse yourself more than if you did not plan at all. You will then be in a position to use that method for most of the time, but you might occasionally use another method if it seems to suit the situation better.

There are many different planning methods, but they tend to be based on just a few basic strategies, and it is those on which we are going to focus here. We will offer you worked examples of each method, followed by some idea of the types of article which each one suits, and some advice on how to use it to best effect.

SPIDER CHARTS

The idea behind a spider chart (sometimes called a spider diagram) is that you can create an argument by looking at various aspects of a situation, but without losing your way in the material. You begin with a central circle in which you place the subject of your article, and then you draw the 'legs' of the spider out from that circle. The 'feet' of the spider, which are circles at the end of each leg, then contain the main sections of your article. To add more detail, you repeat the process of adding legs and feet to each of these main sections.

In the example here we are working on an article that might be entitled 'The challenges and benefits of training for school teachers'. The initial spider chart for this article could look like this:

(Note: 'CPD' stands for continuing professional development.)

This is not a bad start to the plan, but it will need some more work to hone the ideas. At the moment the ordering is absent – what should come first? How will the argument develop? Will all of this material fit into the word count? There is also some confusion at this stage as to the overall shape of the argument, with the benefits scattered in several areas. This is the point at which the writer might choose to restructure some of the material, and might also expand some sections to give a third level of the spider chart. Under the 'barriers to CPD' section, for example, more feet could be added to the 'time' section to consider what is causing the problem (perhaps the curriculum, or teaching and marking loads, or bureaucracy). The 'pupils' section could be renamed 'benefits' so as to make the point more clearly. The writer might also choose to omit whole sections of the plan if they do not, on reflection, seem necessary and the word count is limited. In this case, for example, the writer might remove the 'case studies' section, choosing instead to scatter examples in support of the case throughout the article. This sort of pruning of a plan is often done in discussion with a supervisor or mentor.

It is possible, of course, simply to write the article from this plan, but, as we mentioned in the previous chapter, many writers prefer to take another step first, by transferring the plan to a list of headings and bullet pointed notes. Again, as with the planning method itself, you will need to discover what works best for you, but taking this extra step gives you a further chance to refine your ideas and it allows you to move from a fluid, diagram based plan to a rather more settled, linear plan. In this case, after the further refinements mentioned above, the 'list plan' could look like this:

INTRODUCTION TO THE TOPIC, EXPLAINING RATIONALE BEHIND ARGUMENT

BENEFITS OF CPD

- Pupils see good role models
- Teachers are inspired
- Most up-to-date teaching methods are used → need to provide mechanisms for sharing best practice
- (Pupils can become involved in CPD case studies – relevant? Enough space in article? Ignore if necessary)

BARRIERS TO CPD

- Expense
  - o Who should pay?
- Time
  - o Teaching load
  - o Increased bureaucracy
  - o Crowded curriculum

OPTIONS FOR DELIVERY OF TRAINING

- Training in school
  - Lunchtime talks to share best practice
  - Guest speakers coming into the school
  - Mentoring system
  - Structured free periods for discussion and debate
- External training
  - Formal, advanced teaching qualification (master's degree, for example?)
  - Additional subject training (courses run by local universities and colleges)
  - Skills training (such as sign language, for example)

THE WAY AHEAD: ENCOURAGING CPD

- Promotion
  - Clear, well-recognised promotion structure
- Financial rewards
  - As part of the promotion?
  - In addition to promotion?
- Collegiate support
  - Mentoring system?
  - 'Buddying' system?
- Professional expectations
  - Could be a problem – difficult to change culture – will take time and effort – some detail here as to how it could be begun – good place to end article, looking towards a possible future.

You will notice here that the content has changed slightly. This list plan might be produced after the writer had drawn a second, third and perhaps fourth spider chart, reflecting these changes. You will also see that some subtle changes have taken place. The initial title for the article referred to 'training for school teachers', but for ease of reference in the plan the writer referred to 'CPD', continued professional development. This is only a slight change, but by planning in this way the writer will refer to CPD from the outset of the article, explaining the term and then using it throughout. Had it not been planned in this way, it would have been more likely that the writer would have begun by talking about 'teacher training', then moved on to the term 'CPD' without realising it, and so probably without offering a definition. These little problems can cause an article to look awkward and unformed; eradicating them before they encroach is a further benefit of planning.

Another advantage of planning to this level of detail is that you can see possible glaring omissions. The writer has not included a section about the potential disadvantages of CPD, although one would expect in a balanced article to be shown both sides of an argument. In this case, the writer will probably decide to stick with the plan as it stands. After all, the article title refers only to benefits and challenges. However, even if the writer chooses not to include a section on possible disadvantages, noticing it during the planning stages will ensure the opportunity to mention and dismiss this possibility in the early stages of the article.

Now that we have worked through a spider chart together we can consider its particular benefits.

SPIDER CHARTS WORK WELL IF YOU

- Are going to write an article in which you want to create an argument.
- Think your writing style is a little too note-like and lacks fluidity.
- Are finding it difficult to decide how to order your information and want to see the material laid out before you decide on the ordering.
- Believe that you might have to cut down your material and want to know where to do it.
- Want to use your plan as a discussion document with others, who might change it.

TIPS FOR USING SPIDER CHARTS

- Be prepared to change your mind, and to make additional charts for separate sections of the article if needed. You may well be writing your article from your fifth or sixth spider chart.
- If you find changing a spider chart difficult or irritating, try using 'Post-it notes' for each point rather than writing them on the chart. That way you can rearrange things easily.
- You need to know how far you can go with a spider chart. The example we have given here is the most basic; if you get into the rhythm of using them you may want to add more detail, or symbols, colours and arrows to show how the different points connect to each other and to map out the overall shape of the article.
- Limit the number of initial 'feet' of the spider to the number of main points you can make in an article – rarely more than five or six. If you have too many main points your article might become confused and superficial.
- It is possible to produce spider charts on your computer, but for most people writing on a piece of paper (large, A1 size paper if you like) feels easier and more natural.

A spider chart, as in the example given here, is ideal if you are producing an argument in an article which seeks to persuade the reader of your point. In this case, your overall structure will tend to look like this:

OPENING, TO BRING THE READER UP TO SPEED WITH THE TOPIC
↓
RESEARCH MATERIAL EXPLORED AND EXPLAINED
↓
ARGUMENT DEVELOPED BASED ON THAT MATERIAL
↓
CONCLUSIONS AND/OR DISCUSSION

It is worth noting that spider charts are sometimes called 'trickle-down' charts: they are essentially the same, but the main body of the spider sits at the top of the page, and the legs 'trickle down' the page.

FLOW CHARTS

Spider charts work well for many articles, and are perhaps the most popular planning method amongst writers, probably because of their flexibility. However, if you are intending to write a data-rich article, in which you simply want to offer information in the most logical, linear order, or you want to describe a process, then a flow chart might be a better planning option for you.

Most of us are familiar with flow charts, which are sometimes called hierarchical charts: the only difference between the two is that a hierarchical chart will begin from the top of the page and work its ways down, rather than working along the page from left to right.

To create a flow chart, you produce a series of boxes, with arrows showing the direction of your article, and into each box you write the next piece of information in order to create a logical flow. As with spider charts, you can produce a flow chart on your computer, but be careful. For some people this works well; others find it far more effective to produce a flow chart by hand on a piece of paper. It is really all about how well a computer generated plan will resonate in your mind. You need to feel comfortable with your plan, and remember most of it so that you feel confident as you write, and for many of us a hand-drawn plan seems to achieve this more effectively. Your choice will also, of course, depend on whether you are discussing (and therefore probably changing) your plan with your supervisor or mentor face to face, or long distance by computer.

In the example we will work through here the article title the writer has in mind is 'The effective disposal of chemical waste in the textile industry'. The flow chart for this article could look like this:

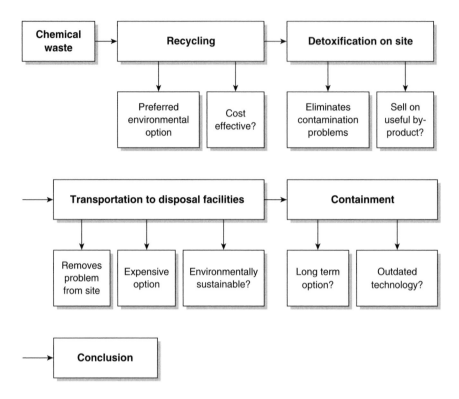

As you can see, the flow chart has allowed the writer to place the options in a logical order, moving smoothly from one option to the next. This method of planning also allows the writer to change this order, depending upon the target readership. If the aim is to persuade the reader that recycling is the best option, the ordering might be reversed entirely, to move from the 'worst' to the 'best' option. Alternatively, if the journal for which the article is being written is a financial journal, then the order can be changed so that the article is nuanced towards cost implications as the key area of interest.

You will already have your target journal in mind and you will have done your research, so you will know how to target that particular readership, but it is worth bearing in mind that a flow chart such as this can be a starting point, to be altered as you research journals.

As with the spider chart, you may choose to move on to a bullet pointed list plan before you begin to write. This can be especially useful if you are to write a data-rich article, as it will allow you to insert data under each section of the article list plan; in this way you will feel as if the article is almost written before you actually begin on the final write-up.

FLOW CHARTS WORK WELL IF YOU

- Are concerned that you might miss out a vital stage in the process you are trying to describe.
- Have all of your data to hand, but worry about how to present it in the most effective way.
- Need to produce a logical flow of information, but feel that you might need to change the order if you change your target journal.
- Are writing for less specialist readers and want to ensure that they can follow your flow of thought.

TIPS FOR USING FLOW CHARTS

- As with spider charts, using 'Post-it notes' instead of writing in the information can make it feel easier to change your mind.
- If you change your ordering, try to do it slowly and methodically: one change is likely to affect the entire chart, so do not let yourself be rushed into making changes.
- It is essential that you leave the chart alone for a while and then check it again before you begin to write. In this way you are more likely to see glaring errors or omissions.
- If you have time, pin the chart on the wall somewhere and keep glancing at it every now and then: this will help you to feel comfortable with it before you write.

Spider charts and flow charts both allow you to make changes to the order and content of your article in the planning stages, but there are times when you need something other than that: you might need help to get started at all.

BRAINSTORMS

A brainstorm is not a complete planning method in itself, but it can be a useful way to get you started and it is both quick and flexible. It begins a little like a spider chart, with a circle in the middle in which you write your general subject matter. Then you simply add random thoughts and ideas around it, in no particular order and with no connecting lines. In effect, you are just transferring every idea you have from your brain to the paper.

Let us say, for example, that you are hoping to write an article on the European Court of Human Rights and its impact on the member states. You have masses of material, but no real idea of how your article might look. You might start with a brainstorm which looks like this:

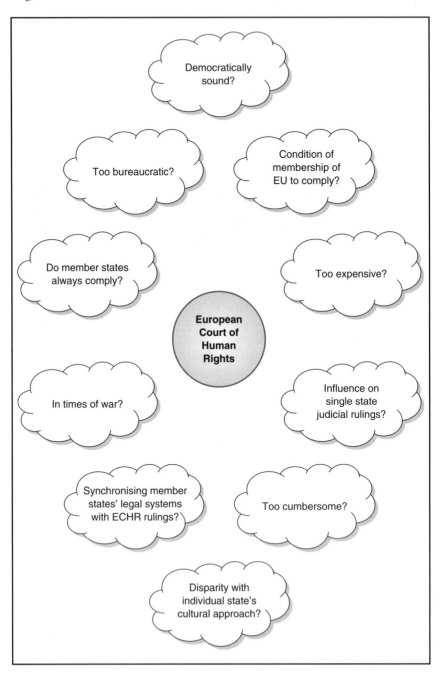

What you have ended up with is a messy piece of paper with plenty of ideas but no order. The next stage is therefore going to be crucial: you are likely to have to reduce the number of points you have included, and you will need to impose order. This is especially true if you are using a brainstorm for a joint authored article. It is an excellent way to help a team to work together, giving even the most self-effacing member of the team the chance to put forward ideas, but someone needs to take control and decide what will, and as importantly what will not, be included in the final piece. In this case, the questions of whether it is too cumbersome and whether it is too bureaucratic are really the same argument, and can be conflated into one point, whilst the issue of whether it can be validated as a democratic entity could be an entire thesis, and may have to be dropped or just mentioned in passing. Similarly, the point about its role in times of war is interesting but not a major point, so it might be mentioned only briefly.

You will thus end up with a pruned version of your original brainstorm from which to move on. In most cases this tends to be a move to another, more complete planning method, although some writers feel comfortable moving from a brainstorm to a list plan.

It is worth mentioning here the benefits to be found in online brainstorming. This works in a similar way to a team sitting around a table to brainstorm, except that it is done by email. You write an email, giving the briefest possible outline of your idea for an article, which you then send around to all of those people who you think might help you to develop the idea. You will need to explain in your email that you do not want more than a few lines back in reply: you are not asking them to labour for hours over ideas or, worse still, try to plan and write the article for you. You can then sit back and await the replies, which should give you the start you need to move to the next planning stage and, perhaps, several ideas for future articles. This is a good way to make use of your email address book, as you will be networking with a wide range of scholars, some of whom you might not have the opportunity to meet face to face.

BRAINSTORMS WORK WELL IF YOU

- Are clear about what you want to include in your article, but have a nagging feeling that you might have missed one obvious point.
- Are struggling to get started.
- Want to encourage discussion at the outset of planning a joint authored article.
- Know that you have too much material for an article, but want to lay it out before you decide how best to cut it down.
- Are trying to find an engaging way to open an article.

TIPS FOR USING BRAINSTORMS

- Be as open as you can in putting down your ideas. Remember that you are not committing yourself to including any of the points in your more detailed plan.
- Keep control of the material: never miss out the stage where you revise the brainstorm.
- Keep copies of old brainstorms. The material you discard from one article could become the idea for your next article.
- Try to keep online brainstorming emails as brief and open as possible so as to receive back a wide range of ideas.
- If you are conducting a group brainstorm, consider including a non-specialist in the group: this often throws up engaging ideas.

MIND MAPPING

There is plenty of mythology around mind mapping, with some going so far as to claim that it can unleash your natural genius by unlocking areas of the brain which are rarely used. It is certainly popular as a revision tool, as it seems to keep facts in the mind very effectively. Here we are not being so ambitious as to try to unleash your genius (you will be doing that for yourself). Instead, we want to consider how mind mapping can work as a planning tool.

A mind map starts off, again, a little like a spider chart in that you place in the centre of a piece of paper the idea for your article. However, as this is a mind map, you will not necessarily be writing in a circle: instead, you might draw a representation of your subject. You then feed off that central idea, showing in words, pictures and symbols, how the article might develop. Unlike a spider chart, there are no spare lines on a mind map: everything joins together in a more organic way so that you end up with a pictorial representation of your article by the end of the process.

The beauty of a mind map is that the process of planning in this way seems to sear the ideas onto your brain, so although making a mind map tends to be slower than constructing a spider or flow chart (not least because you are trying to think of what picture or symbol represents an idea to you), you are less likely to change your mind once it is done, and you are unlikely to forget points as you write.

A mind map is easier seen than explained, so we will give an example here. However, it should be noted that there are as many ways to produce a mind map as there are minds to do the mapping. The example here would work, but if you feel that this is a method which attracts you, it would be a good idea to look at a variety of mind maps so as to get some ideas about how yours might look.

For the purposes of this example we are assuming that the article title is 'Practical measures for downsizing a business during a recession'.

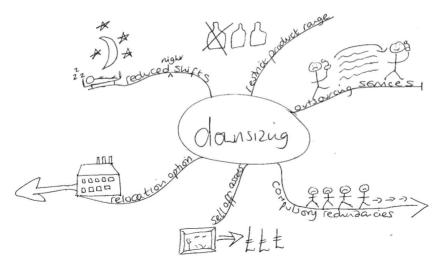

FIGURE 2

As you can see, this mind map is unique: you would be unlikely to use the same pictures and symbols, and you might lay it out quite differently. Perhaps the most intriguing thing about mind maps is that we can all read each other's mind maps, despite each one being so individual. We might not understand every single entry on them, but, as long as we are aware of the context, we can see the general points being made and the overall shape that the article will take.

Mind maps are not for everyone, and writers tend either to love them or hate them. Those who enjoy them tend to become proficient very quickly and it is likely that if you try using one the next time you are planning something, you will know early on whether this method will work for you.

MIND MAPS WORK WELL IF YOU

- Suffer from organisational dyslexia: the barrier of words between your brain and the paper is removed, and so the plan will tend to flow more easily and be of more use to you.
- Want to keep a permanent record of each article you write: all of the detail is there on the page in a relatively small amount of space.
- Have a complex set of ideas to introduce and you are concerned that you might lose your way as you try to plan.
- Tend to rush your planning, and want to slow down rather than finding that you have to keep making new plans as your ideas progress.
- Want to make a quick but comprehensive record of a discussion you are having about how your article might develop.

TIPS FOR USING MIND MAPS

- For each area of your mind map, use at least three colours: we tend to remember better if we have several colours in front of us.
- If you have a mass of technical material to include in your article, do not be put off. A mind map helps you to stand above the detail and map out the overall shape of an article, stopping you from getting lost in the data and so increasing the impact of your argument.
- Try not to become too concerned with your drawing skills as this could slow you down. Only you need to refer back to it, so as long as the pictures and symbols make sense to you, that is good enough.
- Try to fit your writing to the space you have available, so as to avoid any 'spare' lines which do nothing and make it harder to remember what goes where when you come to write.

You now have the tools that you need to plan your article effectively. It might take you a little time to work out the best planning method to use, given the context and subject of your article and the way in which your mind works, but none of the methods outlined here is too time consuming, and the process of finding your best method can be creative in itself, as you hone your ideas and material and bring them to order.

You should now be at the stage where you can begin to write. For some scholars, there is very little gap between planning and writing and they just move smoothly from one part of the process to the next. For others, there is more usually a little break between the two, as they allow the plan to settle in their minds. They are more likely to put the plan to one side for a while, then come back and do a final check on it, to reassure themselves and take an overview, just before they begin to write. Both of these approaches works equally well: there is no 'right' way to do it. However, if you find that the 'little break' is in danger of turning into a prolonged holiday, you might like to read the next chapter.

USEFUL WEBSITE

www.mind-mapping.co.uk

4

COPING WITH WRITER'S BLOCK

CHAPTER OVERVIEW

This chapter will be especially helpful if:

- You find the process of writing too time consuming and frustrating.
- Too often, you find yourself staring at a blank screen, hoping for inspiration.
- You are becoming anxious about whether you can actually produce an article.
- What you write sometimes seems to be of little value, not really expressing what it is you actually want to say.
- At this stage you will do almost anything to avoid having to sit down at the computer and face your article yet again.

In theory, you can move straight from planning to writing; in reality, a significant number of academics suffer from writer's block at one time or another. It can take several forms, from beginning a piece of writing over and over again and deleting the first few sentences each time, to writing whole paragraphs whilst your brain feels slightly out of gear, to staring hopelessly at a blank screen, completely devoid of any inspiration. Two words are important in that sentence: 'screen' and 'inspiration'. We are assuming here that you will be producing your article on a computer, but we are aware that some scholars prefer to write first drafts by hand. If this is the case for you, beware of writer's cramp, which can slow you down. If this happens to you, and your hand and wrist are painful and seizing up, it is worth knowing that writer's cramp comes from the shoulder, not the wrist, so massaging your shoulder will usually remedy it in the short term, whereas shaking your hand around and flexing your wrist might make it worse.

The other key word is 'inspiration'. Frequently, writer's block manifests itself not in an inability to write anything at all, but in the absence of real inspiration: you feel that what you are writing is mediocre or confused. We aim to address all aspects of writer's block in this chapter.

For experienced academic writers, writer's block is a familiar part of life. We come to accept that, on some days, we will just be a little below par, and that what we write is likely to be heavily edited, if not deleted entirely, the next time we come to look at it. If nothing comes to mind, and the screen in front of us remains blank for more than a few minutes, we will take a break and try again later in the day. This is frustrating, of course, but it is part of the creative process and unlikely to be disastrous. For the less experienced writer, the sight of a blank screen, or one which seems to fill up with rubbish, can be downright terrifying.

The impact of writer's block on your life as a researcher might depend on the way in which you work. Some writers plan well in advance and allow some leeway so that they can have days at a time when they do not actually have to produce anything. Others rely far more on last minute inspiration, hoping desperately that writer's block will not hit them. We are not suggesting in this chapter that you fundamentally change the way you work – you will write as suits you best, of course, but we are going to consider with you ways of mini-mising the effect of writer's block.

The first, and most obvious, instruction is, 'Do not panic!' There is nothing fundamentally wrong. Everyone suffers from writer's block at some time or another, and you can put it right. What we are offering here is a range of solu-tions, because clearly it makes sense to try the solution that is likely to work best for your situation. As with so much else in the life of an academic, finding the root cause of the problem is the best way to finding a speedy and effective solution.

You might be suffering from writer's block now, and that is why you have turned to this chapter, or you might want to eliminate possible causes in the early stages of your writing. Whichever is the case, you will need to consider how you feel when you cannot seem to get the words on the screen at all, or in a way that pleases you. Once you have used the chart below to analyse what the cause might be for you, the sections below will give you ideas about how to remedy it.

1 You are just looking at a blank screen, with no inclination to write.

  • Check for boredom.

2 You write a few sentences at a time and then have to take a break; when you read it over your writing seems disjointed and your style is awkward.

  • Check for distraction.

3   You write without any great problem, but then you find yourself deleting most of each day's output, so you end up with a disappointingly low number of words.

 • Check for loss of confidence.

4   You keep revising your writing plan, but cannot quite seem to get anything written.

 • Check for too much information.

5   You have started an article, but you could not find time to get back to it and now you are dreading even the thought of looking at it.

 • Check for heavy workload.

6   You have produced a draft article. It is huge. You have no idea how to reduce it so you abandon it. You start another article. The same thing happens again.

 • Check for loss of focus.

7   You stop writing because you are unhappy with the way in which you are expressing yourself and see no way to improve the situation.

 • Check for loss of words.

1 Boredom

It can come as a nasty shock to realise that, despite the enthusiasm you have for your research area, and the interesting findings which you would like to share with the world, you can feel bored. It is perhaps because this comes as a surprise that we fail to recognise it easily, yet it happens to us all from time to time. The boredom is not, of course, genuinely related to our research, it is likely to have a more prosaic cause.

You might feel this because …

The two most common causes for this block to writing are that you have been working for too long on one task, or that you have lost yourself in a morass of research material and have quite forgotten your leading research questions.

And to cure it …

The easiest option here is to vary the intensity of your tasks. Writing is hard work, both on the brain and the body, so time away from writing can be productive in this situation. You can probably deal with your physical tiredness by taking a constructive break from your work and simply doing something else.

Taking a walk, clearing a few emails or reading for a while can all help, but it is a good idea to time yourself so that the break does not become too extended and you know in advance when you plan to return.

If this physical distancing does not work, and the problem keeps returning, you might need to take more substantial action, by reinvigorating your enthusiasm for, and focus on, your research questions. This might be informal: if you are part of an online research group, or have joined a social network group with other researchers, time spent online now, discussing your research questions and your ideas on how to develop them, can help hugely. You might also consider a more formal approach, such as volunteering to give a brief talk at a research seminar, or calling together a group of your fellow researchers or colleagues with the express purpose of sharing your current ideas. Any activity which allows you to articulate your thoughts and share them with others will remind you of how enthusiastic you are to write about your work.

2 Distraction

This is not a difficult problem to spot, once you have spent a little time reflecting. If you are disappointed with the amount and quality of the writing that you produce in a day, this is the first thing to check. Once you think about it, it will usually become clear. First, look around you. Do your bookshelves unexpectedly look suspiciously neat, perhaps even with the books arranged alphabetically? Is the washing up done? Have you spent time during your writing session on Facebook? Or cleared your emails without really meaning to? If any of this is ringing a bell, you are suffering from distraction, and you are not alone. Procrastination caused by distraction (especially through online distractions) is one of the key causes of underperformance in undergraduates, but it can happen to us all.

You might feel this because …

Some scholars have butterfly brains and for them this will always be a problem. For most of us it is an issue which crops up from time to time, and it will recede with a little effort. One should not overlook the most obvious cause of this problem, which is physical. If you are not drinking enough as you work, or if you have eaten very little, you will struggle to concentrate. Funnily enough, although tiredness is often popularly cited as a cause of distraction, it is not likely to be a problem in the case of writing. We all recall times when we worked late into the night to finish a section of writing for a deadline, or because we had become so caught up in the work, and adrenaline will kick in to help you at those times.

There are, of course, issues to consider beyond the physical. Distraction is often caused by your workload. Not too much work, necessarily, but a wide range of disparate tasks which you are failing to control. If you are writing an article alongside preparing teaching materials, and thinking about a conference paper for next month, and getting enough reading done, and refining your research results, you are going to be distracted. Of course, the list we have just offered is a normal part of the life of an academic: most of us will be writing with at least this number of considerations at one time, before we even think about our lives outside academia. The challenge is not to reduce the number and range of tasks, but to control them so that they cannot distract you as you try to write.

And to cure it …

There is an immediate solution to this problem and a longer term solution. The thing to do straight away is to complete one or two tasks, however minor, as this will help to reduce your stress levels. It should not take you away from your writing for too long, and it will vastly improve your productivity when you return to your computer. Then, when you have completed your writing for the day, consider making a personalised timetable of the challenges ahead of you. This might cover a week, or a month, or even a whole term, but if you can order your tasks so that you know when you have planned to undertake each one, you will find that the gaps you leave as writing time will be far more effective. It is really about giving yourself permission to write amongst all of the other pressing things you need to do in life.

3 Loss of confidence

The tricky thing about a loss of confidence is that it can manifest itself in many ways, from a general reluctance to write, to wishing that you had chosen another topic on which to write, to feeling that you are writing rubbish. The most common effect you will notice is this last: you write in just the same way as you always have done, but none of it quite seems to come up to scratch. You then become frustrated with the subject, with the article, with yourself, but cannot seem to improve your style.

You might feel this because …

You have lost confidence either in your work or in yourself, and it is important to make a distinction between the two. If it is the work which is the problem, you can remedy it in very practical ways. If your confidence in yourself is the problem, you are going to have to make a more concerted effort to work through the problem. It is a strange aspect of a scholarly life that you will rarely find an academic, however well versed in an area, who feels entirely confident: the more you know, the more questions you have, and the more you risk ruining your confidence from time to time.

And to cure it ...

The first thing you need to do is work out if you are, actually, writing rubbish. This is the time to take your courage in both hands and show a section of your draft article to your supervisor or mentor, your colleagues or the critical friend whom we will talk more about in Chapter 6. You might find, though, that even being told that what you have produced is worthy of publication will not dispel your lingering doubts. If this is the case for you, it is confidence in yourself which is lacking, not in the work itself.

There are two key ways to overcome this problem. The first, and easiest, is to go back to the plan for your article and re-ground yourself in what it is you are actually trying to say. This will remind you that you have a brilliant idea for the article and the material at your disposal to make your points effectively. This is one of the major benefits of planning in advance.

If you have revisited your plan and yet still find yourself deleting and/or revising most of your material, you could take a further step towards boosting your confidence, by sharing your ideas with others. This could mean arranging for a well-structured meeting with your supervisor or mentor, where the focus remains on your article, or it could mean taking a break from actually writing the article and instead presenting the material at a research seminar or conference. Once you have shared your material and received positive feedback, it is almost guaranteed that you will feel inspired to write confidently and productively again.

4 Too much information

The problem with trying to include too much information in an article is that you are defeated before you even start to write. You make a plan, but it does not sit as neatly as you had hoped, so you revise your ideas and make a new plan, which still seems inadequate. Before you know it, you have several rather muddled plans in front of you, and you have not written a single word of your article. The trick to solving this problem is to recognise that it is not the plans which are going wrong: it is simply that you are trying to squeeze several articles' worth of ideas and material into one little article.

You might feel this because

Until you have written several articles, it is extremely difficult to know how much material is the right amount for an article of any given length. There is also a natural tendency to approach your first few articles almost as if they were examinations designed to test your knowledge, and your response to this is to try to include far too much information. You are anxious to impress, and yet you are hindering yourself unintentionally.

And to cure it …

Go back to your research questions for the article. Do you have too many? How many is too many? Check out other articles in your target journal and analyse them: how many research questions do the article writers tend to pose and answer in each article? If you ignore the brief research questions towards the end of an article, which point the way towards a future research direction, you will probably find that it is just one or two. Do you have more than that? If you only have one principal research question but it is huge, consider narrowing it down.

Once you have the perfect research question for your article, consider how much material you need to include in order to be able to answer it. Readers (and editors) of journal articles are interested in your ideas and theories, backed up by enough material to make them credible. Think back to your research process. You may have a mass of material now, as you have tested and retested your hypothesis over time, but how much did you need to make you believe that you were correct in your suppositions? However much you needed, this is how much the reader of your article needs.

What you are aiming for is to engage the readers but leave them wanting to know more about your research and about you. You are not expected to write the 'last word' on a subject in an article. Indeed, experienced researchers know that the 'last word' does not exist in any field.

A side benefit of producing an article that is incisive and engaging but not overly full of a mass of evidence without adequate interpretation is that, if you are not writing as if you think you know all the answers, you are more likely to be contacted as a result of the article, or because someone recognises your name at a conference and offered other ideas from more experienced scholars in your area. A colleague of ours always refers to writing journal articles as 'fishing trips'. He produces the article and sits back to assess the result, which usually involves queries from other scholars about what he is doing and how they might work with him on a problem, or approaches at conferences from those who are keen to offer their own ideas to add to his hypotheses. This seems to us to be a productive way to view articles, and certainly inspires us to 'go fishing'.

5 Heavy workload

This is not writer's block at all in the true sense of the term, but it can be just as burdensome. It is not that you are unenthusiastic about your subject area, or having any especial difficulties when you come to write about it, but you seem to start and stop, endlessly. This makes writing an article seem like a mountain to climb, so that when you do come to write you feel under pressure and your writing style begins to suffer. What could have been a constructive, even enjoyable, writing experience has become no more than another chore to be completed.

You might feel this because ...

The simplest, and most obvious, answer is that you are simply overworked at the moment. Our work (and home) lives fluctuate, and sometimes we do not have time to spare for anything much beyond the absolute basics of life. The challenge here is to know whether it truly is overwork which is preventing you from writing, or something more complex. It could be that your workload is fragmented and unbalanced, so that it appears to be heavier than it is, or perhaps your life outside work is preying on your mind too much, so that you struggle to concentrate and spend too much time worrying at the expense of writing.

And to cure it ...

Try to avoid any assumptions about the problem, but instead produce a personalised timetable of the tasks you have to complete over, say, the next six weeks. Include both work and research tasks and those challenges you face outside work. If you have a critical friend, supervisor or mentor who could help with this, all the better. Once you have completed the timetable, analyse it to see if the answer lies there. If you are trying (or are being forced) to fit too much into life at this stage, and it all seems to you to be absolutely essential, abandon the article for a time, if you can. It is far better to leave the article idea or plan to one side for a few weeks and then come back to write it when you have allocated sufficient time to it, than to struggle through and be dissatisfied with everything you write.

This leads us to the question of how much is 'sufficient time', and this is a good point at which to analyse how you work. Some scholars work more effectively by allowing themselves small blocks of time in which to write, some find this very difficult and are only comfortable if they have set aside several days as 'writing days' with few interruptions. By thinking through how you work best, you will be guided as to how to plan your writing in the future, once the immediate pressure is off.

There are two dangers here. First, it might be weeks before you feel you have sufficient time to focus on your article. In addition to setting it aside for the present, you must decide at what point you can return to it, and stick to that plan. Second, you must decide whether the problem is really one of over-work, or whether in fact you simply have a workload which is too fragmented (perhaps you have an awkward teaching or learning timetable for a time, or you are on too many committees and research groups, or your research has reached the point where it is engaging your thoughts to a greater extent than normal). A fragmented workload, or poor life balance, can be remedied to some extent, but this is a long-term challenge, and in the meantime you may have to produce a personalised timetable which sets aside *some* time for writ-ing. It might not be the ideal length of time for you, but writing even a small portion of an article and then leaving it to one side, confident that you will come back to it at the time indicated on your personalised timetable, can be far better under these conditions than writing nothing at all for the foreseeable future.

6 Loss of focus

Some article writers tend to worry in the early stages that they will not have enough material to fill an article. In reality, the opposite problem is far more likely to arise, when an article becomes too long and loses its focus. This leads to an unwieldy article and a writer who is wrestling with it. The frequent response to this is to stop writing for a time, hoping that it will sort itself out in your mind, and then to find it very difficult to go back to the article to rewrite or revise it.

You might feel this because …

This tends to happen for one of two reasons: either your research question is too wide, or you have become so bound up in your research, so committed to your ideas, that you cannot bear to do anything less than include abso-lutely everything you have learnt into one article. This approach leads not only to an unmanageable article, but also to a great reluctance to cut any-thing out of it. In cases such as this, writing too much is as problematic as writing too little, and the result is the same: an article which is not ready for publication. The danger here is that you might then struggle to write any-thing at all, feeling that you have 'failed' in article writing and so will fail again in whatever else you write. This problem always needs to be solved as speedily as possible.

And to cure it …

This is where planning can help you enormously. Rather than simply giving up (which is unlikely to be a realistic option) or labelling the article a failed attempt and ignoring it, you can use a plan to rescue the situation. Skim read your article and make a plan as you go which reflects the main structure of the article. A spider chart or a mind map is often the best planning method to use for this (see Chapter 3). Once you have a plan in place, it is a relatively easy task to revise the plan, extracting whole sections which are not essential so that you end up with a far smaller plan. You can then remove whole sections from your article, safe in the knowledge that what you have left will make your point effectively. The remaining article can then be polished and edited into shape.

There are dual benefits to this plan of action. Not only will you end up with a far more focused article, you will also have several unused sections of your original article, which might very well end up being the starting point for your next article.

7 Loss of words

Words are strange things. We use them all the time, confident that we can express our ideas clearly and effectively, yet we rarely give them much conscious thought. In an article there might be a paragraph or two where you really agonise over getting the words right, because it is an important section of your argument, but in general you will simply write and trust that you are writing well. It is for this reason that it can be so unnerving to find yourself writing in a way which displeases you.

You might feel this because …

We all write in a less than impressive style from time to time, but in the case of article writing it is usually more a case of the wrong type of vocabulary than anything else. This has probably happened because you have been caught up with a different type of vocabulary, such as the one you use for teaching or preparing for a conference, and so your style and expression reflect that experience rather than being appropriate to the journal in which you hope to be published.

And to cure it …

For such a distressing form of writer's block, the answer is surprisingly simple. Immerse yourself in the journal which you are targeting. Do this little and often, ideally several times a day. The subject matter of the articles you read is irrelevant. It is the style, tone and use of words which are of interest to you. Within a few days you will find that you have got into the habit of thinking more in this style, and you will then naturally write in a way that is more in keeping with your target journal.

It is worth pointing out here that your own writing style is a valid expression of your ideas and so you need not aim simply to try to copy slavishly the style of another writer. It is more a case of absorbing a general type of style and vocabulary used in a specific journal. The idiosyncrasies of your writing style will still be there to some extent, and this is a good thing.

SOME REMINDERS

If you suffer from writer's block in the future you will probably return to this chapter for guidance, and we are aware that you might need no more than a quick reminder of how to remedy it, rather than reading a whole section again, so we are including here a table of reminders.

1 Boredom

- Eat and drink.
- Take a structured break.
- Share your ideas.

2 Distraction

- Complete one or two tasks, however minor.
- Produce a personalised timetable.

3 Loss of confidence

- Return to your plan.
- Share your draft article.
- Present some of your ideas in other ways.

4 Too much information

- Reduce the number of research questions.
- Reduce the breadth of your research question.
- How much research material do you actually need?

5 Heavy workload

- Use your personalised timetable.
- Analyse the true nature of the problem.
- Learn how you work best.
- Carve out some writing time.

(Continued)

(Continued)

6   Loss of focus

  - Retrospectively plan your article.
  - Remove extraneous sections from the plan.
  - Revise your article in keeping with your new plan.

7   Loss of words

  - Immerse yourself in your chosen journal.
  - Read little and often.
  - Allow your writing style to form naturally.

A WORD OF WARNING

It is worth noting here that, although we have gone into some detail about the symptoms and causes of writer's block, it is too easy to assume that you have a serious problem when in fact you are simply following a natural pattern of activity. We all undulate through writing, sometimes slowing down, and perhaps showing some of the symptoms given here, and at other times speeding up. Rather than becoming overly concerned that you might be suffering from writer's block, it is far better to accept that we all need a short break or distraction now and then. As I wrote the last section of this chapter, a perfect example of this occurred. My phone rang. I answered it, but the call was not for me and so all I had to do was take a message. Nevertheless, I knew the caller and so we chatted for a few minutes. Although I was not aware that I had begun to slow down in my writing, showing signs perhaps of some of the symptoms of writer's block, I was very conscious that my writing speeded up considerably after the phone call. A useful lesson to us all: sometimes you are not suffering from incipient writer's block at all, you just need a short break.

SOME QUICK FIXES

The solutions we have suggested above will take some effort on your part, but there are times when you need a quick fix which will keep you writing in the short term, even if you need to address a larger issue for the long term. With this in mind, we are suggesting here some ways to 'ambush' yourself, so that you can keep on writing regardless.

  - **Keep a 'rubbish' document permanently available on your computer.**
    If nervousness or anxiety is getting the better of you and keeping you from getting started on your article, or you feel that you are writing well below

your best, a document permanently kept on your computer entitled 'rubbish' can help. This takes the pressure off you. When you write in that document you know that you are not committing yourself to the real article, and so writing becomes easier. You will often find that when you come to look at it after a time, what you have written is far more impressive than you had anticipated, and you can copy it into the article.

- **Write – anything.** Writing is a creative process, and one that needs to be nurtured. If you are finding the idea of writing your article daunting, then producing some synopses of articles you have recently read, or preparing some teaching material, or producing a short written presentation for a research seminar can all help to keep your writing fluency ticking over until you feel confident enough to begin on the article.

- **Try writing in pencil, or vary your font style.** It is interesting to note that, despite the fact that academics tend to use just one of two fonts (Times New Roman or Arial), we still each view these fonts as if they were our own handwriting, as if somehow they are unique to us. You can use this to your advantage. If you use another font (or, if you prefer to draft in handwriting, a pencil rather than a pen) you will free yourself from the responsibility of trying to write a 'perfect' article. It feels more like doodling, and your words will come more easily to you.

- **Keep a notebook near you at all times.** This technique works brilliantly for some, not at all for others, so you could try it. The idea is that you can record your ideas as they come to you. This is especially useful if you tend to have great ideas shortly before you fall asleep. You might find that much of your article is there in draft form when you review your notebook.

- **Plan until you can write.** Planning is a great way to get your ideas into order and to develop your hypotheses, so you need not restrict your plan to just the bare bones. If you are reluctant to begin writing, refine and develop your plan. Make it as detailed as you can, including bullet points for what you want to say in each section, a few facts or quotations which you know must be included, even the occasional sentence which strikes you as you work. As your plan becomes very detailed, you will feel as if you have almost written the article before you have even begun, and in this way you can lure yourself into writing.

- **Try recording yourself.** If putting words on the screen (or page) seems like too much of a commitment, simply speaking into a recording device can relieve the pressure. Talk through your plan, expanding it as you go into full sentences, then type up your recorded notes as a basis for your first draft. As with all of these quick remedies, it might work well for you or not work at all, so you will need to see this as experimental.

- **Impose artificial but realistic deadlines.** The success of this technique will depend upon the sort of person you are. The idea is to force yourself into writing. There is rarely a strict deadline imposed on producing an article, often there is no deadline at all, so you could impose your own deadlines. This might be simply writing in your diary which sections you need to complete by certain dates, or making a detailed personalised timetable in which you include sections of your article as tasks to be completed. Some writers find this very useful, and stick to their deadlines rigidly; on others it has little effect. Again, it is a case of trial and error to see what works for you.

- **Produce a word or time target for each day or week. Increase it over time.** Writer's block is sometimes more subtle than simply failing to produce any words at all, as the detailed sections above explain. If your problem is that you struggle to produce enough high-quality words (and this can be a huge and persistent problem for some scholars) then giving yourself targets can help. You can impose a specific writing time on yourself each day, or a number of words to be completed each day. This latter can cause problems, though, as most of us tend to write naturally in sections or to complete a certain number of thoughts, rather than to a word count, so for some scholars a word count target can be off-putting. It is best to start slowly, with perhaps half an hour a day or a couple of hundred words, and then build up over time until you feel that you can spend enough focused hours at a time simply writing and producing a reasonable word count.

In the popular perception, writer's block tends to be associated with writers of great novels, or lengthy theses, but it can be far more of a challenge for those producing articles. You need to impress in a relatively tight word count, and this is bound to produce a level of pressure that can cause problems. However, writer's block has, perhaps, an unfair reputation. It is seen generally as an entirely negative affliction, put amongst us to frustrate our best efforts to achieve our desired results. If you are in a hurry to write, it can be a nightmare, but for those of us with some experience of writing (and so, inevitably, more than a little experience of writer's block) we come to recognise its potential as a positive aspect of our writing lives. If we are afflicted with writer's block we know that we can use the techniques detailed here to cure it, and if it plagues us for some time we would take action, but we are equally likely to let things be for a little while. Some days are simply not good days for writing, and that is fine. There is always plenty more to be done, and we know that the next time we face the computer screen with an article in mind, it will transfer itself easily from brain to fingertips, and we will be back on track.

5

GETTING THE STYLE RIGHT

CHAPTER OVERVIEW

This chapter will be especially helpful if:

- Your last serious piece of writing was your thesis, and you suspect that your writing style has become too expansive.
- English is not your first language.
- You are not sure about the structure required in a journal article.
- You have become lost in a morass of research data.
- You tend to struggle to see your writing as a reader, rather than as its writer.
- You want to improve your writing style generally.

YOUR WRITING STYLE

We are making some assumptions in this chapter as to the general level of your writing. We assume that you can write reasonably well in a formal academic style, and what we hope to assist you with here are some of the specifics of journal writing (such as writing an abstract) and a few common problems in writing which can catch out even experienced writers. If you do not feel that you have reached a standard of writing which would show your ideas off in their best light, you may want to do some work on improving your writing overall, but the most important aspect of writing for you at the moment is that you *know your writing*. You will need to be analytical about your current level of expression, and for that you need some honesty.

Some of this honesty will come from you. Think back to comments you tend to receive on your written output, bearing in mind that you might have to go back some way to find closely annotated work which you produced, perhaps to your undergraduate essays or dissertation. Very often researchers receive the same feedback time and time again (for example, your 'writing style is vague' or 'you need to work on your grammar') and never seem to get the time to work systematically through the problem in order to improve their style. Within their day-to-day lives this might not matter: their colleagues and supervisor can understand what they are trying to say and so the problem is perhaps a nuisance at times for those reading their writing, but no more than that. Although one could argue that a journal will have copy-editors and proof-readers who will work on articles in order to raise them to the necessary level of accuracy and formality in writing, it is still important to present the best possible case for your article, and this includes making sure that the writing is as accurate, and as elegant, as you can make it.

You can also ask for honesty from your supervisor, mentor or colleagues. This is not an easy thing to do if you have already worked hard on your article; the last thing you might want to do is to have to rewrite sections or go through correcting minor mistakes. It can also be a little awkward. You are used to discussing your ideas and your research material with these colleagues, and your writing style will not necessarily have hindered that process at all: to have to ask them now to look at your writing abilities can make you feel vulnerable amongst your peers, but it will pay dividends once you receive constructive and detailed comments upon your writing.

You also need to be honest with yourself about the process. Do you find writing burdensome, or does it come easily to you? Do you tend to spot mistakes or would you prefer to rely on someone else to check your work through? Are there aspects of writing which you have always meant to check out but never seem to have done it? Do people tend to praise your writing abilities or do you often find yourself having to rewrite so as to make your point effectively? Most of us know how well we write, and how much help we might need, and this is the time to assess just how much you need this chapter before you read on.

This chapter is divided into three broad sections: the structure of your article, the detail of writing well, and how to check and polish an article prior to submission.

IF YOU ARE WRITING IN YOUR SECOND LANGUAGE

If you are not writing in your first language, it is easy to become anxious about your writing style and how well it might reflect both your research and your professional image with a journal editor. In reality, this rarely causes problems, but you need to be clear about what you can achieve. Some aspects of writing tend to cause problems which are highly intractable, such as confusion over the use of the definite and indefinite article ('the', 'a' and 'an') and the correct use of prepositions. These can remain problematic even for experienced writers over many years, and they signal nothing more to an editor than that you might be writing away from your first language. They will not hinder the progress of your article and are easily corrected by copy-editors and proof-readers.

For aspects of writing such as this you can relax, refusing to let such a minor problem ruin your confidence in what you are trying to do. However, if you know that you have a more serious problem expressing yourself accurately and fluently, this could be disastrous for what you are trying to say to potential journal readers. Again, you will need to seek the honest opinion of your supervisor or mentor to be able to establish whether you do have a problem in this area.

In the early days of your career as a researcher, you might want to invest occasionally in the services of a technical editor, who can ensure that your writing reflects your work in the best way possible. It may be comforting to know that you will not need to use this service for very long. Our use of language is an organic process. You can learn much from books and by receiving formal instruction, but it is only by using the written language regularly and enthusiastically that you will improve: and you are likely to improve far more quickly than you had expected.

The secret to increased fluency is thus simple: write, write, write! Take every opportunity you can to express yourself in writing, and ask for help as you go. Realistically, your supervisor or mentor may not have time to proof-read every single piece of writing you produce, but others can help. We often encourage our research students into 'skills swaps', whereby one student will, for example, regularly proof-read the other's writing, in exchange for help in other areas of work. This allows for an informal exchange of expertise and is one of the quickest routes to improved writing style.

THE STRUCTURE OF YOUR ARTICLE

The abstract

This is clearly going to be an important aspect of your article, both in terms of enticing the reader and making clear your intentions to a journal editor. It could be called the 'sales pitch' for your article. It will be word limited, but journals differ on the words allowed to abstracts so make sure you know the word limit *before* your start to write it: it is a nuisance to have to rewrite it if you change your mind later about how many words you have at your disposal.

In terms of content, you will need to go back to your target journal to see if you are being offered express instruction on what to include. If you are not given instruction, then look through a whole series of abstracts to see how they are being approached. If you check out your journal online you may find that abstracts for back issues are offered separately, which would allow you to see a series of them easily so that you can get a good idea of what is expected of you.

An abstract is not necessarily a summary of the article in its entirety. It may simply be a way to indicate an area of research to the readers, or to give an indication of why the article has been written, or where it might go in terms of methodology and problem solving. Before you assume that you have to encapsulate your entire article into a brief abstract, check on what it is intended to do within the journal.

Abstracts are frequently used for electronic keyword searching. Indeed, in some fields this is their primary use. You will need to find out how your abstract is likely to be used, and how you can satisfy the requirements of your target journal. Keywords may be included (perhaps in bold) in a narrative abstract: that is, an abstract which indicates the content of the article to your readers. Alternatively, they may not form part of the abstract at all, but instead be listed after the abstract as a separate entry. An abstract, in some cases, might be no more than a list of keywords, waiting to be searched online by those interested in your field. Again, find out how (and if) you are expected to include keywords.

If you are basing your article on work for which you have previously written an abstract (such as a conference paper), try to avoid the temptation simply to reuse the abstract. You will have targeted it towards a particular audience for a particular occasion, and there is no guarantee that it will fit your article. You could keep it near you for reference, but a straight replication is unlikely to work.

Researchers are sometimes encouraged to write an abstract last, as the final task in producing an article. This is a logical approach. By that stage you will know exactly what you have written and be in a good position to précis it into an abstract. However, we are not convinced that this is necessarily the best approach. It is often extremely difficult to reduce an article to an abstract once it is written. You will be tempted to try to include too much detail, because you have just written the detail, and you may even resort to copying and pasting entire sentences, which are likely to be far too expansive to suit the neat and succinct style of an abstract.

We would advise instead that you use the abstract as a test of your understanding. If you have produced a detailed plan and are at the point where you feel ready to write the article, having thought through all of the challenges ahead of you and firmed up in your mind the arguments you want to make, you should be in a good position to write your abstract. If you find it difficult, getting muddled and struggling with the word count or how to express yourself clearly, this will give you a useful prompt to go back to the planning stage and rework your material until you feel confident about writing your abstract.

If you write your abstract in this way, it will not necessarily be the final version. Inevitably as you write the article it will nuance a little and your finished article will not be exactly as you envisaged it in your plan, but once it is written, returning to your abstract will be a pleasure. Spending time making minor changes to your abstract and polishing it to perfection will be a satisfying experience at this stage: an intellectual reward for a job well done.

The introduction

We would approach an introduction in much the same way as an abstract: if you cannot write it straight off at the start of the writing process you are probably not clear on what you actually want to write for the rest of the article, and need to go back to the planning stage before you begin.

As with the abstract, your introduction might vary according to the article, but also according to your personal style of writing. Some article writers like to give what is, in effect, a conclusion in their opening paragraph, whilst others prefer only to give a hint of their conclusions and then lead the reader with them through the body of the article until they reach the conclusion together. Both approaches can be equally effective, but we offer you here a checklist of material which you should consider including in the introductory section of your article:

- An explanation of the title of the article: is the reader clear on what you are aiming to achieve in the article? Have you given a clear outline of the journey you are about to make together?
- Your area of expertise: why are you (or why is your team) well qualified to write this article?
- Your sphere of reference: this is the scope of the article, giving an indication of what areas you intend to cover in the article.
- What you do *not* intend to include: although this properly comes within the scope of the article, we highlight it separately here as it is so important. You do not want to have a distracted reader who is waiting for some material to appear which you have not included, so you need to be clear on this.
- An overview of the material, which should give the reader a firm idea of the background to the project or issue which you are about to discuss in detail.
- How your argument will develop: this is a structural pointer. You will not be trying to précis the entire article, or rehearse the arguments in detail in advance, but an indication of the general thrust and structure of your argument will help the reader to remain focused throughout the piece.
- A sense of your conclusions: as we have already suggested, this might be no more than a hint of where you (and the reader) will end up by the conclusion of the article, or you may choose to point out your conclusions more fully at this early stage.

This may seem like a lot of material to cover in an introduction, especially in an article which is limited in size, but each of these points need take no more than a sentence or two. You may not need to include every one of these points, but you do need to produce the introduction with them in mind, and only exclude them if you know you have good reason to do so.

The article on the page

You may be in the lucky (or nerve-racking) position of having no particular word count assigned to your article, but this would be rare in a peer-reviewed journal. There are two ways that you could expect to be given a limit to your writing: by word count or page length. As we discussed in Chapter 3, a word count is something into which you must relax to some extent, ensuring that your plan is supportive of the word limit for which you are aiming, and then allowing the article to develop naturally, adjusting the word count in the later stages of editing and polishing.

A page limit can be a far more challenging experience, and it is a common enough requirement for us to consider it here. The advantage of a page count is that you can use all of your textual options to prise the material into the required number of pages, and you are likely to produce an article which uses graphs and charts, bullet pointed lists and tables, and a smaller font size than you might usually experience. The problem for you as the writer is that a page count can make your writing, and thus your thought processes, feel cramped from the outset. You will be trying to eliminate the 'white space', which is a natural feature of most of our writing, in order to fit the page count, so your margins become smaller, there is less space around tables and charts, there is a temptation to create fewer paragraph breaks. This can lead to a dense writing style, with clipped sentences and thoughts which are either abbreviated, or not followed through as you might normally expect to do. This is obviously not a good position to be in as the writer.

Luckily, the solution to this insidious problem is simple: ignore the page count as you write. Your plan will naturally lead to approximately the right length of article, that was part of the point of producing such a detailed plan, and so you can let your writing flow naturally. Once the article is complete, copy and paste it into a new document and then, if you need to, begin the task of reduction by reformatting, reducing white space and so forth. If your article is still too long once you have been through this process, you will need to cut it down by editing your writing. At this point, *do not* try to work from your second, reduced copy, but go back to the original that you produced. You will know by approximately how much you need to reduce it, but by working on the original, rather than the more cramped looking version, you will avoid the temptation to alter your writing style in a way that could be detrimental.

You will then have to copy across your reductions and corrections into the reduced article, but if you print out a version which has tracked the changes you have made this need not take long. Once you are at the stage where you would like to give the article to your supervisor or mentor for comment, and perhaps some proof-reading, offer it in the original format rather than the reduced version. It is far easier to proof or edit an article in a twelve-point font than having to peer at it in a ten-point font. Of course, for the article reader the reduced font size will not be a problem, but for those who are scrutinising the article in its early phases it can be.

Signposting and structure

We could happily write an entire chapter dedicated to the art of signposting in your writing, but we intend to focus, for the purposes of this guide, on two aspects of signposting: signposting words and signposting sentences. The idea behind signposting is that you include words or sentences which do not add anything substantial to the meaning of what you are trying to say, but instead help to guide the reader through your article. One way to do this is to consider using signposting words and phrases. Some of these will include:

- 'However', 'therefore', 'in conclusion': these indicate to the reader that something is about to happen. In the case of 'however', you are about to make a turn in your article from stating one position to qualifying or con-tradicting it in some way. In the cases of 'therefore' and 'in conclusion' you are reassuring your reader that progress is being made, or alerting the reader to the fact that a high level of attention is needed as you are about to bring the strands of your argument together.
- 'Whilst', 'whereas', 'although': whenever a reader comes across any of these words at the beginning of a sentence, it is a clear (but largely subliminal) indication that a proposition will be put forward at the opening of the sen-tence, which will later be qualified or contradicted at the end of a sentence (after a comma).
- 'Further' and 'furthermore' can add momentum to your writing, enticing the reader through your article as you add more and more layers to your argument. However, overuse can be a problem. Nobody wants to read an article in which every paragraph opens with these words, so be sparing in your use of them.
- 'If': the use of 'if' at the beginning of the sentence usually tells the reader that it is necessary to consider the first point offered in the sentence and decide whether it is acceptable before moving on to the second point being asserted.
- 'It is both': this phrase can add a sense of balance to your article, suggesting that you are being judicious and weighing up all sides of an argument. It should not be overused, but is a powerful tool when used sparingly.
- 'At the end of the day', 'at this moment in time', 'at this present moment': these phrases give the reader a clear indication that you have no idea of exactly what you want to say, or how to express it, and should *always* be avoided.

Now would be a good time to establish how well you signpost your writing. Having offered you some words and phrases to get you on your way, take a highlighter pen and check a recent piece of your writing. Highlight the words that you can see do no more than guide the reader on the page. Whilst you would not want to tax the reader with signposting at the expense of content, it makes sense to ensure that you have a good sprinkling of signposting on the page.

Signposting sentences are used in part to guide the reader forward through your article, but are used even more effectively as a means of reassurance. Your plan will ensure that your article flows through a natural progression of stages. You are likely instinctively to introduce each stage with an opening sentence which effectively tells readers what is about to happen to them. Too often, inexperienced writers forget to include the second piece of signposting, at the end of each section. This would be a sentence or two which summarises what you have just written in that section. You cannot, of course, encapsulate everything in just a sentence, but you are not required to do this: you simply need to summarise the detail enough to allow the reader the chance to think 'Oh, that is not what I thought you were saying at all' and then go back to reread the section. This form of signposting is not always easy to do as you write, but it is a simple enough task to include these sentences when you come to check and review the article in its early draft form.

Presenting technical data

You will be offering your reader plenty of material in your article, and if this is not highly technical data, you will often do it in narrative form. That is, you will simply explain what you have discovered and lead your reader through the material you have gathered in the same way that you then explain the conclusions you have drawn. If you are including technical data, especially if it is complex or copious, you are likely to include charts, graphs, tables and such like.

In the early stages of an article your readers are keen to work through the material as they try to grasp the basis on which you are going to draw conclusions and because you have just given an introduction which makes the importance of the data clear to the reader. However, once readers have reached about two-thirds of the way through an article they may flag a little. Your hypothesis has become fairly clear, and seems well supported by your evidence, so there is less of a sense of urgency to grasping the technical data. There is also, perhaps, a distracting sense that the reader is coming towards the conclusion of the article and rather wants to get to the end. Both of these factors can lead to less attention being paid to data, particularly very complex or challenging data. It is not possible, of course, for you to counter this tendency simply by putting all of your data at the beginning of the article, although if you have a choice about positioning in terms of what you are writing, you might want to favour the inclusion of technical data early in the article. Beyond this, ensure that you 'cushion' the data more the further through the article you are. This simply means including a sentence or two at the beginning of the later sections of your article which reiterates why the set of data which is about to appear is important, and why you have included it. This is also, incidentally, a useful test for you. If you cannot sum up why you have included some material, you will be forced to question whether you need it there at all.

Textual options

We have been discussing in this section the use of several textual options, such as bullet pointed or numbered lists, graphs, charts, tables and so forth. A word of caution: make sure that this is an acceptable form of presenting information for your target journal. It will be in a scientific journal, of course, but in other journals there might be a trend against such textual options, or even a requirement to limit or abandon them. If no explicit guidance is offered to you on this point, go back and look at back copies of the journal to see which type of article is favoured.

If you are using these options it is usually far easier to format them in your draft article as you would normally do and make changes as needed in later versions. Journals have their own way of formatting lists, or indicating tables, or laying out other insertions, so be ready for these changes before publication. If the changes are made by the editorial team after acceptance, do not assume that a slight change of format will have no effect upon the content: always check these thoroughly to make sure that your material is still there exactly as it needs to be.

Concluding your article

As with so much to do with writing, producing an effective and memorable conclusion is largely a matter of personal choice and style. You will produce a conclusion which best suits your article, but you might want to consider two points: a conclusion should usually be brief and should almost write itself. You will not want to waste your word count on re-rehearsing the arguments you should already have made convincingly. You will also want your conclusion to arise naturally from the body of your article. If you find yourself labouring to write it, or it is becoming unwieldy or unclear, then stop writing. If you go back to your detailed plan and ground yourself back in what you have said, you will then write your conclusion with more confidence and clarity. This is a useful technique, in fact, whenever you feel that your writing is becoming unclear. Rather than simply glancing back at what you have just written, which might confuse you even more, check your plan and then start writing only once you have your argument clear in your mind again.

THE LANGUAGE OF YOUR ARTICLE

Good English is always simple English. It is writing which is to the point and elegantly flowing, by a writer who does not use six words where one would serve the same purpose, and equally a writer who does not use one jargon or highly specialised word where several simple words would suffice. Good English is produced by a writer who prepares well and is clear about the needs of the reader.

Your readership

We will address this last point first: you cannot know the level of expertise of every single reader of your article, nor could you be expected to know, but you are required to write with consideration for the needs of the ostensible readers of the article. That is, those readers for whom the journal is intended. This is going to be crucial to the success of your article and is, for most of us, one of the most difficult aspects of writing of any sort. You must remain aware of your reader throughout the production of the article, right down to the last checking stages, and you simply must resist the temptation to do no more in your article than show your brilliance at the expense of the readers' understanding of your points, or to become so enamoured of your research that you lose any sense of a reader in your delight at reworking your material.

You can always assume that, whatever category of reader you will encounter, you will be catering for a potentially international audience. This does not require wholesale changes to your writing style, but you do need to be aware of this dimension to your readership. It will require you to avoid national clichés: for example, we have tended to use the word 'encapsulate' in this chapter rather than the more colloquial and less widely understood phrase 'in a nutshell'. It does not, however, ask that you avoid any word that might not be readily understood by every reader: for example, we use the word 'gargantuan' later in this chapter, safe in the knowledge that it is relatively widely understood and with the confidence that our readers would be prepared to look up the occasional word if they are unsure of its meaning.

This outward facing approach, which is one you will always have to take in writing journal articles, comes more easily to writers with experience, until it feels natural to write with this focus, but there are steps you can take now if this is likely to be a problem for you.

STEP 1

Consider the readership of your journal and categorise it on a narrowing scale: is it a general readership (the widest category), a more narrowly defined readership, a readership in your field but not necessarily within your narrow field of expertise, or an expert readership well versed in your specialist area? It could be that readers from all of these categories will use the journal, and your default position should be to write to the widest range of readers according to this categorisation. Thus, if you know that your target journal is used predominantly by general readers, you will have to cater for their needs. This does not prevent you from putting highly specialist material in the article, but you will need to provide an adequate explanation of the material so that even the most general reader can appreciate your argument, even if not all of the fine detail.

STEP 2

Try working from your plan to produce a presentation of your article, by preparing all of the slides you would use in a presentation and then actually standing up and giving the presentation, imagining the audience members as the type of readers you would expect to be using your chosen journal. Once you are happy that you could make your points effectively and intelligibly to this audience, print off your slides and use these as your detailed plan for the article.

STEP 3

Ask colleagues or friends who you think are representative of your target readership to sit in a group and listen as you read your article out to them. Ask them to stop you whenever they are unclear about what you are trying to say, either because your writing style has become too dense, or you are using unfamiliar jargon, or using terms in a way which is unfamiliar to them, or bombarding them with too much (or too little) information. Mark the points at which they stop you in your article and then go back to consider whether you should make changes in the light of their level of understanding.

Writing simply

We are not suggesting here that you write simplistically, with short sentences and a dull vocabulary which would appeal to nobody, but we are suggesting that you are clear enough before you begin to write that you can express your thoughts without using so many words that you, and therefore your reader, gets tangled up in them. You are also likely to put a reader off entirely if you insist on using jargon which is not well understood outside your field of expertise (or perhaps, as sometimes happens, outside your own research team). There are several ways to ensure that your writing remains as simple as it needs to be whilst still engaging the reader.

Try varying the length of your sentences. Resist the assumption that short, snappy sentences are always to be preferred. It is quite difficult to write persuasively if you only use very short sentences, but it can be difficult for your reader to follow your point if your sentences are always gargantuan. Work through the first section or so of your article, counting the number of words in each sentence and jotting down the number. You will end up with a tally of numbers which should show a good range, with the majority of your sentences containing between (approximately) twelve and twenty-five words, but with some pleasing variation either side of that range.

Include plenty of paragraph breaks. Paragraph breaks are hugely reassuring to the reader, as they are a natural 'escape point' at which the reader can pause and consider what has just been said, whilst preparing for the next paragraph. If your article looks too dense, paragraph breaks include some useful 'white space' into your writing and increase its accessibility without you actually having to do any rewriting at all.

Use your textual options. As we have already suggested, textual options such as bullet pointed lists and visual depictions can help to make your article clear and persuasive. Lists act in a similar way to paragraph breaks, allowing the reader some mental space to consider a point before moving on to the next one. Graphs, charts and so forth allow you to encapsulate complex information in a relatively simple to grasp form and give the readers a rest from the text.

Use headings. Again, you will have to check whether your target journal offers any guidelines or imposes strictures on this, but a heading or subheading can be an influential signposting tool, allowing readers to grasp the overall shape of the article at a glance, and alerting them to a new topic area.

Look out for your favourite words. We all have terms we love to use and that we find comforting. Certain words and phrases just seem to convey exactly what we want to say, or we like what they say about us. The first of these uses is desirable, as long as you resist the urge to use it three times in every paragraph. As soon as you sense, as you type your article, that you are repeating a word, jot it down somewhere. When you have completed the article, use the 'find' function on your software to see just how often you have used it, and then change it to an equally apt word in some of those instances. We are suggesting that you do this as part of the checking process, because it is surprisingly difficult to think of another word to use as you write, and can be an unnecessary distraction, but once you check back it will be easy to think of a perfect substitute word.

We all have a tendency to use words for what they say about us, and this is both natural and desirable. If you can find the perfect word for your purpose it is to your credit, but erudite words can be strangely addictive. They make us feel intellectual and well versed in our subject, sometimes at the expense of our readers, who not only fail to understand our meaning, but who also resent us for confusing them in this way, and suspect that we are enjoying ourselves a little too much at their expense.

Improving your style

There are three techniques which will always help you to produce good writing:

Read articles

This may sound simple, but it really is the best way to ensure that your mind is working along the same lines as other journal-article writers. By immersing yourself in articles you will naturally adopt a more appropriate style of writing, with the right level of formality and reader focus.

Plan thoroughly

We have suggested this already, but planning is the only way to guarantee that you are not thinking too much about *what* you want to say at the expense of *how* you are going to say it. The planning process gives you all the time you need to think through the article and to change your mind: it is a highly creative process. You will know when the time to write has come, because you will feel a strong urge to transfer your plan onto the page by beginning to write. If you can wait until this moment comes before you write, you can be sure that you are in the best possible position to write well.

Reading aloud

In order to assess how well you write, and thus improve your style, you need to become a reader of your work. It is surprising when you come to think about it: writing is one of the few activities we do where we cannot see the end result. Of course, we can see the writing on the page, but we cannot see it as a reader will receive it, and this is always the end result of our writing. So, take a piece of your writing (ideally three or four pages) and read it aloud to yourself. Do this walking around a room, keep a steady pace, and really work on the expression. Pause at each comma, take a longer pause at a semi-colon or full stop. Become the reader. You will be startled at the result, because for the first time you will be experiencing your writing as a reader does. As you 'walk through' your writing in this way, keep asking yourself how you sound. Do you sound excited, in control and authoritative, or do you sound bored, pompous or anxious? The tone of your writing will become clear to you as soon as you begin to read aloud, and mistakes you have made will seem to jump off the page and make themselves obvious. You will not need to read everything you write out loud in this way, but it is good practice to do it every now and again, and certainly your journal article will benefit from this treatment.

EDITING YOUR ARTICLE

We refer on several occasions in this guide to the need to be ready to edit your work. This is not the same as checking and polishing your article (to which we refer in the next section of this chapter), but is a more radical process. You will be editing, most usually, so as to make significant changes to the length of your article.

Increasing the length of your article is a relatively easy task, because an under length article is usually lacking something in terms of material. It might sometimes be the case that a scholar writes in far too clipped and note-like a style, but this would usually be picked up by a supervisor or mentor before that scholar begins to produce articles. In the more usual instance of there being insufficient material, your editing task is relatively straightforward in the first stage of the process. You will go back to your plan and take an overview of the piece, considering any sections which you cut out in the planning stage and deciding whether, in fact, they should be included.

The second stage is a little more challenging. Having decided to include some extra material, you will have to read through the whole article in order to ensure that it still works as a complete piece of writing, that it does not refer to material which is now in a different place, or fail to mention some item which is now an important aspect of the article. It is, of course, best to avoid having to undertake this laborious task, which is why we urged you to check with your supervisor or mentor as to whether your plan seemed to them to include sufficient material for your article.

There is one word of caution with this type of editing. All new material should be necessary to your article: avoid throwing in a plethora of material which is not really needed, just so as to reach a word count. Similarly, avoid at all costs the temptation to become wordier and less clear simply to 'fill out' the article. If the word count is too low and yet you feel that the content is absolutely right, avoid simply tinkering with it. If necessary, change the title to indicate a wider remit and rewrite the article under this new title, rather than risk producing an artificially inflated article which has lost its immediacy and impact.

As we have already suggested, editing in order to increase word count is relatively rare. Far more common is the need to edit in order to reduce the word count, and there is a step-by-step system by which you can do this.

STEP 1

If your article is seriously over length, go back to your plan (not the written article) and examine it with a view to deciding if any sections can be safely discarded without detriment to the whole.

If you find that you can do this, remove those sections from the article, but remember that you will then have to go through the whole piece to make sure that you do not refer to that section anywhere else.

This is a painful process but it might enhance your article significantly, if you find that you have included a stray section which should really have been removed at the planning stage. If you cannot find an obviously extraneous section, stand firm at this stage whilst you consider the other steps you could take to précis your work down.

STEP 2

Even if you decide that you have to include all of the sections contained in your plan, there may still be sections in your writing which are superfluous. This sometimes happens because we get led astray by our enthusiasm as we write, and sometimes it is the result of offering information that seems important at the time of writing, but becomes redundant as the article progresses.

Work through your article, as swiftly as you safely can (to avoid getting tied down in the detail) and mark up any sections which you feel you could exclude, or significantly reduce, now that the article is complete. Again, this should feel like a positive process. You are tightening up your article and increasing its impact.

STEP 3

Consider all of the textual options open to you. To some extent, this will depend upon your discipline area and the journal for which you are writing, but if you have the opportunity to include word saving options such as bullet-pointed lists, or graphs, charts and tables, now would be a good time to consider them.

Using textual options such as these not only saves words, because you can easily encapsulate a whole paragraph in one small chart, for example, but can also be of great benefit to the readers, many of whom will find it easier to grasp information in this form.

STEP 4

You will have already decided, in Step 2, whether there are sections of your article which need to be removed altogether. Now you have the pleasure of spotting, and tidying up, any sections which are needed but are far too cumbersome.

We call this a pleasure because you are not asking yourself at this stage to go through the uncomfortable process of actually removing material from the article, but rather giving yourself the chance to make it more elegant. Skim read it (as fast as you can go without losing the sense of the writing) and mark with a highlighter pen any sections which you can see, upon this more mature reflection, are too wordy. This will tend to have happened at points where you felt unsure of yourself, either because the material would not sit quite naturally into the point you were trying to make, or because you were tired as you wrote.

These sections, once marked up in this way, are usually easy to improve. If there are not too many of them, it is usually easiest to rewrite the entire section rather than fiddling about with it.

STEP 5

In some ways, you want to avoid this step, as it is not designed to improve either the content or style of your article, but is simply a technical and potentially time-consuming process you might have to go through in order to conform to a word or page count. Having said that, it can be quite a pleasant intellectual challenge and, if done well, it will take nothing from your article, either in terms of its impact or message.

If you are down to the bedrock of you article, knowing that every point in there must remain, and all of the material you have included is vital to support your argument, you have the option of working through each sentence in order to précis it down. This is done by removing words which are not essential to your meaning, replacing phrases with just one perfect substitute word and removing phrases and sentences which you can see are not absolutely essential. It is amazing how effective this can be: we all use potentially superfluous words all of the time, and this is often to the benefit of our style, but a stripped down, elegant writing style can also work well, even if it does not come naturally to us at the writing stage.

POLISHING YOUR ARTICLE

Writers are sometimes advised to read their piece of writing through twice, from start to finish, in order to find and eliminate mistakes. In our view this is the worst possible way to check, because you are reading the piece as you wrote it, and will necessarily find yourself reading what you thought you wrote, rather than what you actually wrote. In addition to this, you will become bored with the writing very easily and so will tune your mind out from the task. We have already pointed out that you need to move away from your text in order to become more like its reader than its writer, and some physical space at this point is a good idea. Leave the article to one side for a while (ideally, several days) before you begin to check it.

Once you are ready to begin on the art of polishing your article, it usually works best if you can follow an established system of checking and polishing and use the same system each time you undertake this task. The system below works well.

FIRST CHECK

For this check you need to move through the article at some speed. You are not making a detailed check, but rather getting a sound idea of the overall shape of the article and how well it works as a whole. To make sure that you are checking at the right speed, you should be able to read the odd word and phrase, but not complete sentences: you are just focusing on the whole. If you have turned your spellchecker off because it kept throwing technical words which it did not recognise back at you, remember to turn it on again before this stage, just to ensure that you will not come across too many irritating typing errors as you check.

(Continued)

(Continued)

As you work through the article at a relatively brisk, steady pace, have a highlighter pen beside you. When you spot one of the features we mention in the checklist below, make a note in highlighter in the margin, but do not stop to correct it yet. Check through the whole article before making any corrections, asking yourself these questions:

HAVE YOU PUT ONLY THE NECESSARY MATERIAL IN THE ARTICLE?

When you spot a dense section of complex material, just consider for a moment whether you actually need to include it. Of course, in most cases it will be essential to what you are trying to achieve, but at this stage you are in a good position to judge whether it is effective as it stands, or whether you need to reduce its bulk or, perhaps, present it in another way so that it helps the reader's understanding rather than hindering the smooth flow of the article. If changes need to be made, put a large 'M' in the margin beside the problem area with the highlighter pen, to indicate that this material might need to be reworked.

DOES THE INTRODUCTION MATCH THE MAIN BODY OF THE ARTICLE?

If, as we suggested, you wrote your introduction first, you may find that you added a few ideas to your article which were not in your plan, so now is the time to put a large 'I' in the margin whenever you come across such material, so that you know to go back later and amend your introduction.

IS THE FORMAT CONSISTENT THROUGHOUT?

Because you are not reading through in huge detail, it is easier to see if there are points where the look of your writing on the page has gone awry. If you have changed font size for subheadings, or italicised something where elsewhere you have emboldened the text for a similar item, this will become obvious to you at this stage and you will be able to place a large 'F' in the margin to remind yourself to make changes.

IS EVERYTHING CLEARLY LABELLED?

It is common enough to find articles being submitted where the author has simply failed to notice that an insertion of some sort (a table, graph or chart) has not been labelled correctly. If you spot this insidious little mistake, an 'L' in the margin now will ensure that you eradicate it before submission.

HAVE YOU INCLUDED ENOUGH 'WHITE SPACE'?

If you are not page limited for the article, you will want to make it as accessible and appealing to the editorial team as possible. This usually involves leaving plenty of white space around textual inserts, and decent sized margins, and plenty of useful paragraph breaks. 'WS' will be needed in the margin whenever you notice that your article is looking too cramped on the page. Of course, changes will be made to the layout of the article by the editorial team later, but at this stage your principal goal is to present your work in the best possible light.

DOES IT 'DIP' TOWARDS THE END?

The only time you might slow down a little in this first check is when you are about three-quarters of the way through the article. We all tend to make silly blunders when we are three-quarters of the way through writing a piece, perhaps because we are distracted by realising that it is nearly complete. Rather than using your highlighter in the margin, for the few paragraphs at this point in the article, check it in detail, before moving back to your more general check for the rest of the piece.

ARE YOU BEING FAIR TO YOUR READERS?

It is always frustrating to decide to dedicate an hour of your life to reading someone else's view of a subject, only to feel let down by the end of the article because you have not really understood the points the writer is trying to make, or grasped the essential argument. When you realise that this has happened because the writer has obscured the meaning in a poorly written article, your frustration tends to turn to irritation, and you will remember the writer's name as someone whose writing is to be avoided in future.

As the writer, you clearly want to avoid this disaster, so at this stage you must be firm with yourself. As you go through this first check, highlight any words which are obscure or ambiguous (you will not spot them all at the speed at which you are working, but some will jump out at you). If you have used an abbreviated term and failed to define it, highlight it. If your flow of argument, now that you are taking a view of the whole article, is patchy in places or seems to have missed out a stage, highlight it. Once you begin on the second stage of checking these things will not be so readily spotted, so try to eliminate them now.

Once you have made this first check of the article you will be left with a piece of writing which is potentially very good, and certainly capable of being far better than it was. This thought will sustain you as you incorporate the changes and corrections required by your highlighted notes to yourself.

Having made the first batch of corrections and amendments, you would, ideally, leave the article to one side again for as long as you can before you make the second check, but this is not essential if you are pushed for time.

SECOND CHECK

The second check is the time to delve into the detail of your article, but we are still not suggesting that you begin by reading through from start to finish. Instead, take it in sections.

IS THE ORDERING LOGICAL?

Take a look at all the headings in your article or, if you have written it without headings, jump through from section to section with just one question in your mind: does it flow logically? Have you offered your readers an easy path from one point to the next, so that they can take the journey with you and reach the same conclusions?

ABSTRACT INCLUSIVE ENOUGH?

This is the stage in the writing process when finessing your abstract should be a pleasure. Now that you have taken a look through your whole article in brief, do you need to add anything to the detail of your abstract to make it perfect?

ABSTRACT BRIEF ENOUGH?

Once you have added a few points to your abstract, it might be too long or perhaps not quite as flowing and authoritative as you would like. This is your chance to rewrite the abstract in its entirety, if you feel this is needed, confident that you are clear about every aspect of the article and what you are trying to achieve.

HAVE YOU BEEN OBJECTIVE?

Whilst the act of writing is, necessarily, a subjective process, you will want to reassure your readers that you have taken care to look at all sides of an argument and weighed up all the disparate evidence at your disposal. As you sit back and consider the article, can you think of any points where you might have left your reader wondering 'yes, but what if...?' You will not want to rewrite your article, but you might want to insert a sentence here and there which acts as a signpost, reassuring the reader that you have considered a point, and then discarded it for good reason. You do not want a reader who is distracted by an uneasy sense that something potentially vital is missing.

ARE YOUR CONCLUSIONS ABSOLUTELY CLEAR?

As you wrote the article, you would understandably have been at your most tired when you came to write your conclusions, and it is easy to lose confidence at such a crucial stage of the article, leaving this as a weak section. You might have tried to include too many conclusions, just to avoid criticism, leaving the reader with the difficulty of trying to ascertain which are the key conclusions (if there are any) and which are of far less importance. Your writing style might also have dipped, so that you have tended to become too wordy or too concise, or adopted a style of writing which lacks confidence. You now have the support of the whole, impressive article behind you and can rework the concluding section. If you need help to gain clarity, check back to your plan to clear your mind and ground yourself back in exactly what you were trying to achieve.

IS THE DETAIL RIGHT?

This, finally, is the point at which you read the article through once, from start to finish, with an eye to the detail. You have moved away from it since you wrote it, and the checks you have made so far will have distanced you even further, which will help you to spot mistakes far more easily.

DOES THE TONE WORK?

As you make this final check, keep a 'tone monitor' in your mind. Are there points at which the tone has slipped from confident, enthusiastic and in control? If you find them, now is your chance to rewrite them

IS IT RELATIVELY READER PROOF?

Take a step back again and think about you article overall. Many different readers will have access to your article, some with more expertise in your area than others, some with a better grasp of research methodology than others, and some with a keener intellect than others. The experience of reading your article will differ for each of them, and this is as it should be. Whilst you cannot be responsible for every reader who happens across your article, you are responsible for ensuring that every single reader can at the very least grasp the main thrust of your argument. The detailed material may pass them by, the complex methodology be a mystery to them, but the main points which you are hoping to convey should be open to all. In any well-written article, all readers, of average intelligence and education, should be able to work their way through it and understand at least the overview of your argument. That is what your final check is aiming to achieve.

We are aware that we seem to be suggesting an awful lot of work here. Surely, you may ask, it would be easier simply to read the article through twice from start to finish, as you were told to do at school? Actually, once you get into the rhythm of checking using this system it takes no longer than a laborious read through time and again, and it is a far better way to spot mistakes. An editorial team is about to see your article, and although it will inevitably make some changes, this checking system gives you an excellent chance of presenting a clean, coherent and impressive article.

At this point, things should be so simple. You have read this guide, written your article, polished and checked it, and now all you need to do is to send it off. For many writers it *is* that simple, but for some this transition is not nearly so easy. In the next chapter we will explore with you why you may find the next move difficult, and how you can overcome the problem.

USEFUL WEBSITES

http://oxforddictionaries.com
www.plainenglish.co.uk/crystal-mark.html

6

LEARNING HOW TO STOP WRITING YOUR ARTICLE

CHAPTER OVERVIEW

This chapter will be especially helpful if:

- You have spent much too long on trying to write an article and this is getting in the way of your other research commitments.
- You feel haunted by an unfinished article.
- Every time you look at your journal article, it seems to be less worthy of publication.
- You have several half-finished articles stored on your computer, all waiting for their finishing touches.
- Your article has been keeping you company for so long that you know you will feel bereft and aimless once it is finally complete and submitted.

WHY YOU NEED TO STOP

It can all seem so simple at the outset. You write an article and you send it to your chosen journal. This is easy. Except, of course, that it is not necessarily simple or easy at all. Journal articles can linger, clinging to the hard disk of your computer in a semi-complete state and apparently resisting all attempts to complete them and actually send them off.

To some extent, this is a normal part of the life of a scholar. All of us are involved in numerous projects all the time, and so we become quite used to allowing half-completed projects to rest for a while as we move on to other, more urgent tasks before coming back to complete the journal article, or book, or new teaching module, or whatever it is that has lingered for a while. This is, perhaps, one of the key differences between being an undergraduate and moving on to become an established scholar. Throughout your early education you became used to completing a task, submitting it for appraisal and moving swiftly on. As a postgraduate that rhythm of work stops, forever, and this is a good thing. It is a new way of working and one that stays with you for as long as you are an academic. However, there are three good reasons why, in the case of writing journal articles, you need to complete the task, stop and move on.

Losing your sense of the article

After some initial checking, the more you review, revise and polish an article, the more it is likely to look wrong. You can begin to see problems with it which simply are not there, and so you keep on polishing it, losing confidence with every review, until you can no longer tell whether it is a good article, which reflects well on your work.

Losing your way

There is a danger that you will never get it finished. This may seem incredible, given that you have purchased this book in order to learn how to produce an article which is then published, but it does happen, far more often than you might think. Undergraduates often talk at graduation about the few books which they meant to read throughout their time at university, but never quite seemed to get around to finishing, or even opening. Scholars do just the same sort of thing, but with the articles they meant to complete, the conference papers they fully intended to give, and the book proposals which never moved beyond the 'good idea' stage. If you lose your way, and can no longer see whether the article is really finished, or still in the primary stages of being polished, you may give up altogether and file it away, ready to begin on yet another article which you feel sure you can finish – until it, too, is consigned to your pending tray.

Losing your sense of yourself

From the outset of our postgraduate careers, we are all gaining a sense of ourselves as academics. Your ostensible goals will change: gaining your doctorate, perhaps completing a post-doctoral project, moving on in your career. However, along this journey you will learn surprising things about yourself: perhaps you are an unexpectedly good administrator, an impressive speaker, a fantastic team leader or an inspiring teacher. These are all gratifying things to learn about yourself, but less pleasing is the sense that can grow on you that you cannot seem to write journal articles. This will not be true, but if your early attempts at writing articles drag on for months and months, just because you cannot seem to stop, you will be left with a feeling that the task is monumental, and this will make approaching each new article much more difficult.

EXERCISE

If you are struggling to complete your article, it will be knocking your confidence already, so now is a good time to remind yourself of what you have already learnt about your talents. List here three areas of your academic life in which you know you can excel (the paragraph above might give you some hints):

1
2
3

If you can do all of this, completing your article is just one more thing that you can do well.

WHY YOU CANNOT SEEM TO STOP

The first thing we should do here is to reassure you that you are not alone if you have a few articles sitting around in various stages of being written, from those which are little more than a list of 'good ideas to include' to those which are within an inch of being complete. We would like to think that you are in good company, as we, too, have unfinished projects waiting for our attention. It keeps you motivated to know that you have exciting projects in the pipeline, so this is a good thing. We both know that we will never have enough time in our careers to complete all of the things we want to do (many academics find this) and have already decided that we probably need files marked 'for retirement' so that we can work on these projects when we finally have more time (this is why academics often struggle to retire completely).

Not seeing the wood for the trees

If you have a multiplicity of tasks and projects in hand, it is easy to become confused and convince yourself that you simply do not have the time to spend on completing an article and polishing it up ready for publication. In reality, you probably do have the time, but you cannot see where it can be found. By being clearer about the tasks before you, you will be able to prioritise more easily and so find a gap to work on your article.

EXERCISE

It is useful to consider what other projects and tasks you have in hand, as a muddled list of 'things to do' might be blocking your way to completion. You could probably list dozens of things here, but try to concentrate on key tasks and major projects. List six of these here, and include your journal article:

1

2

3

4

5

6

The secret of succeeding is not necessarily to limit the projects which you have in mind, but to ensure that *most of them are completed* as you go along. Now that you have itemised the challenges you are currently facing, you might well be able to see that your journal article is the easiest task to complete. Luckily for all of us, journal articles provide the perfect project for completion. You are not relying on anyone else for completion (even for jointly written articles you can complete your section). They are nicely self-contained, rather than being part of a larger project, and once it is complete, you can send it off.

It is not you, it's me

For some scholars, the problem is actually nothing to do with the article itself. It is about the sort of person they are. Some people just find it difficult to complete anything. Just this morning we received an email from a mutual friend who tells us that he is staying abroad for the next six weeks, during which time he will complete two book chapters and five articles. Having received a similar email for the last few years, we are fairly sure that he will return home with the *beginnings* of all of these: completing them is a much less secure assumption. The friend in question is a great 'ideas person', always coming up with new ways to teach old modules, fresh ideas about how to tackle challenges and inspiring thoughts about the way forward in each new situation.

Indeed, he is so keen that he frequently makes unnecessary work for himself, which he then has no time to undertake, and will begin new projects on an almost weekly basis, very few of which will come to completion.

The problem here is twofold. Our friend is easily bored, and so always looks for a new challenge, and he is unable to convert his initial excitement over a project into the determination needed to see it through. For him, the final outcome is far less important than the idea of inception. Innovators such as this are, of course, hugely important in the academic world, which relies upon original thought and superb new ideas. However, it also needs 'finishers', who can follow through on those ideas, and as a writer of journal articles you need to be both, to some extent. By learning whether you are an innovator rather than a finisher, you will be in a good position to know that you need to apply all the techniques offered in this chapter if you are to complete the job. There are psychometric tests you can take to discover the type of person you are, but the questions below should give you some clues:

EXERCISE

1   If you are reading this at home, as you look around you do you see several small maintenance jobs around the place which you never seem to get around to?
2   In meetings, are you the outspoken one who inspires everyone, and then hopes that someone else will actually do the legwork?
3   Do people tend to approach you in the hope that you will find a creative solution to their problem?
4   Do you love to plan a holiday, perhaps even a little more than you actually enjoy going on the holiday?
5   Do you become impatient with people whom you consider to be too plodding in their approach to a project?
6   Do you file product guarantees and instruction manuals without actually reading them?
7   When you are in a group, do you usually see the best way forward quickly, and then have to wait for others to catch up with you?

If you have answered 'yes' to most of these questions, you are probably an innovator rather than a finisher, so reading this chapter is a good move for you.

It just feels good

There is something about being able to say 'I am writing a journal article' that feels satisfying. You can confidently say you are doing something, you can feel that you are making solid progress, without having to produce the finished product. This is bound to boost your confidence in the short term, but after you have been saying the same thing for months and months you will start to find that the process reverses itself. You have committed yourself. Everyone knows that you are writing an article, but you have not done more than the first draft, and begin to feel tremendous pressure to complete. As a natural response to this, you are actually less likely to be able to complete. This chapter is going to help you to break that vicious circle, so that you can know how good it feels to say 'I have just had an article published'. The first stage in this process is to consider how it would feel to be able to change what you say to others.

CHANGING THE LANGUAGE

1 'I have an idea for a journal article' could easily become →
   - 'I am producing a plan for a journal article'.
2 'I am drafting a journal article' could easily become →
   - 'I have completed the first draft of a journal article'.
3 'I am writing a journal article' could easily become →
   - 'I have asked a colleague to look over my draft article'.
4 'I am polishing a journal article' could easily become →
   - 'My article is good enough to send off'.
5 'I have nearly completed a journal article' could easily become →
   - 'I have sent it off to a journal publisher and am awaiting reviews'.

When you come to consider the statements above, you will see that the differences in what you are doing are, in reality, very small, but by forcing yourself to change your language, you will see the process differently, by giving yourself permission to move on to the next stage. What we say to others has a profound effect on what we do and how we behave, so aiming to be able to change your language can be a very productive way to ambush yourself into moving ahead to reach completion.

Going public

It is an often bemoaned fact that academic research can be an isolating experience, as you work alone on assessing your research material and testing your research hypotheses. Whilst this is certainly a valid point, to see it as an entirely

negative situation is to overlook the luxury of time and space which this position offers you. Particularly in the early stages of your academic life, you are
able to work alone on your own ideas, deciding how best to articulate your
thoughts and present your findings. There is nobody there to push you unduly,
or to criticise your half-formed hypotheses. You can take your time and you
have the mental space to get it just right, to ensure that the work you produce
is a perfect representation of your best thoughts, your most exciting ideas and
your most original findings.

This is an extremely seductive position. You can become so wedded to the
idea of your own private space for thought and expression that offering your
writing to anyone, even your supervisor or mentor, can seem like an invasion
of that space. Once anyone else reads your article you are inevitably open to
criticism, however constructive this might be. Once you come to see, as we all
do in the end, that no article can be perfect, that no idea is ever complete in
and of itself, and that all of your findings are inherently open to scrutiny and
further development by others, it is easy to become reluctant to show anything
to anyone.

You will overcome this hurdle. The process of scrutiny by others is the life
force of academia; it is what generates new ideas and ensures that we all produce the best possible results. Nobody ever writes a 'perfect' article: we are all
just as good as we can be at that moment. Our articles reflect our thoughts to
date, our findings as they are now, and our hypotheses at just one stage of testing and scrutiny. However difficult it is in prospect to share your writing with
others, it is not until you allow your work to become part of this process of
scrutiny that you will truly become an academic, and that brings with it a new
sense of excitement.

LEARNING HOW TO STOP

Having spent some time analysing why you might find it difficult to stop and,
we hope, convincing you that you must stop, solving the problem is surprisingly simple. We offer here some techniques which will allow you to write
your article, scrutinise it as objectively as possible, and then send it off.

Time away from the process

Simply reading your article over and over again is not going to gain you a clear
perspective on it; you need to walk away, leave it for a while (ideally for a week
or so), and then come back and read it again, straight through, as if you were
the reader of a journal. In that way you are far more likely to see afresh just
what you are trying to say, and how well your points have been made.

Becoming a reader of your work

As we have mentioned before, in Chapter 5, it is surprising to think that writing is one of the few things we do for which we cannot easily see the result. If you paint a picture, you hang it on the wall and admire it just like everyone else. If you plant a seed, you can watch the plant grow. Yet, you write an article and you are writing into the ether. Unless you become a proficient reader of your work, you cannot hope to judge it as others do. For this, you will need to read it out loud, so as to alienate yourself from the text and be able to judge it objectively. It will feel strange to do this, but we are suggesting that you walk around a room, reading your article fairly slowly and with as much expression as you can muster. What you will get from this process is a sense of the overall shape of the article and an idea of whether the tone is right. You will also see glaring mistakes which you are unlikely to have spotted had you not read it aloud.

It is what friends are for

Throughout your academic career it is a good idea to use a 'critical friend' for your work, perhaps someone for whom you can return the favour, if you are both writing regularly. Ideally your critical friend will not share your specific area of expertise, and so will be in a good position to view your writing dispassionately. This is the first stage in transferring your work from your private space of thought into a wider arena. As you hand your article over, try to avoid the temptation to spend ten minutes anxiously explaining what it is you are trying to say. Simply pass it over with as little comment as possible and see what your critical friend thinks of it.

A critical friend is a very special person: both words in the term are important, and the balance between the two is essential. It should be someone you trust to be impartial and offer constructive criticism, but also someone with whom you are friendly enough to take the criticism without feeling hurt or souring your relationship. So, not too friendly, not too critical, but a good blend of both.

When you are writing an article you are, quite rightly, utterly immersed in your subject area, and it is easy to overlook the obvious, because you fall into the trap of thinking that readers will know exactly what you are talking about, even though you have not actually told them. One of the authors of this book remembers vividly the first time she handed an article over to her critical friend. It was only when her friend asked her to which historical period she was referring that she realised she had forgotten to put in the birth and death dates for any of the historical figures about whom she was writing. With a friend, this was an amusing oversight; with a reviewer or editor, it would have been acutely embarrassing.

A gift for your supervisor

Articles can be a delight to supervisors and mentors. Having worked with a postgraduate researcher or research colleague on the minutiae of a project, and waded through reams of research material, plans and draft chapters or papers, to sit down and enjoy an article is a real pleasure. It gives your supervisor or mentor a sense that progress is being made, and a glimpse of how the final product of the research project might shape up. The work might not be entirely new to your supervisor or mentor (you will have shared your early plans for an article) but when you can hand it over in its 'final' form, at a point where it has probably become stale to you, it will be fresh and engaging for your supervisor or mentor. In this way, you can expect comprehensive feedback as well as comments upon the detail.

Insight through conferences

We suggested earlier in this book that you might use material prepared for conferences as the basis of articles, and so here we are offering a word of caution. Whilst conferences can be the best place to inspire ideas for articles, and to hone your ideas into a workable form, taking a 'finished' article to a conference and giving it as a paper or presentation can cause problems at this late stage. Given the nature and purpose of conferences, your article will inevitably be cause for discussion, debate and queries. However brilliant your article is, this process is likely to raise doubts in your mind about how good it really is and whether it is actually ready for submission. So, whilst in the early stages a conference can be extremely helpful, in this much later stage it could be counterproductive.

AND THEN NOT REALLY STOPPING

Having spent an entire chapter of this book trying to persuade you to stop working on an article once you have completed it, we will now appear to contradict ourselves completely. You will, naturally, breathe a huge sigh of relief when you send your article off to a journal editor, but this is not the final stage in the process, and nor should it be. There are going to be more stops on the journey: receiving the editor's initial response to the article, working through reviewers' comments and making any necessary changes, working with an editor or editorial board and, finally, checking the article prior to publication. This is all to the good, but it means that you will be living with this piece of writing for some time to come.

Showing your 'finished' article to a critical friend and your supervisor or mentor are the first little steps in making your work public. You will probably find that it was not the 'finished' article at all, as you will have made some changes as a result of their comments. However, you have to trust that it is, now, as finished as it needs to be before you send it out into the world. We discuss elsewhere in this book how to deal with editors' and reviewers' comments as positively as possible, seeing them as a new group of 'critical friends'; here we will consider for a moment what else you might be doing as your article continues on its journey.

Once you have submitted your article to a journal, it begins a new phase, as it is read by others who will consider its value and, more importantly, decide if it is a good fit for your chosen journal. Of course, there is nothing more you can do at this stage for that article, but it is entirely detrimental to your state of mind if you just sit back and await the result of this scrutiny. The reviewers will probably be busy academics who will work on their review whenever they find the time, and the journal editor will be involved not only in perusing other articles for issues months ahead, but also dealing with preparing the current issue of the journal for print. All of this takes time, and it is time that you cannot afford to waste. In addition, if you are pinning all of your hopes on one journal and waiting to hear back on a daily basis, your heightened state of anticipation is likely to lead you to respond far too emotionally and, perhaps, negatively to any feedback which you are offered.

So, stopping altogether is not a good idea, but you may feel little enthusiasm for launching yourself into another article when you have just submitted one. This is a natural response, and will resolve itself in a relatively short space of time, but there is also a more insidious problem which arises for many less experienced writers. It is sometimes said that everyone has one great novel in them. This might be true, but it is certainly not the case that we only have one article in us, although it can feel like this when you have just submitted your work. After all, you have completed an article which included many of your best ideas to date, used up large amounts of your research material and seems to you to be the last word in your area. Except, of course, it is not the last word, nor is it *your* last word.

This can be a scary time. You flounder around, anxiously awaiting a response from your chosen journal, wondering if you will ever have anything else to say, and finding yourself distracted from the everyday tasks ahead of you. This is obviously not a productive state of mind, but there are simple steps you can take to ease yourself out of it.

There is never just one article …

Imagine for a moment that we are both standing in front of you, refusing to let you leave the room until you come up with ideas for your next few journal articles. It is 4.00 pm on a Friday afternoon, you are dying for a cup of tea, and you want to leave by 4.30 at the latest so that you miss the rush hour traffic on your way home. You also have six library books to return before you leave, and one urgent email to answer about a meeting on Monday morning. Oh, and we have only given you a pen and paper and none of your research material to look at. And we look really mean.

Now we have you in the right frame of mind, jot down below the three ideas for journal articles that have just popped into your mind. They do not have to be perfect, or polished, or even necessarily brilliant, but they do exist in your head and writing them down here will convince you of that. One of them might even become your next article.

EXERCISE

Ideas for an article:

1

2

3

There is never just one journal

For you, just now, it might seem as if there is only one journal of any importance, the one to which you have submitted your article. However, if you have followed our advice to research journals in your area thoroughly, you will know that there are others which might be interested in an area of your work. If you continue to carry out your research, regularly checking what is being included in your target journals, and perhaps spotting what is coming up in future issues, you will achieve two things. You will keep your mind focused on future publication possibilities (you cannot leave it too long before you produce your next article) and you will be reading the work of other writers regularly which will help to improve your writing skills by reminding you of the style of writing required for journal articles.

You might also like to consider other journal possibilities. Although peer-reviewed, specialist journals in your subject area are your principal target for publication, there will be other opportunities open to you. You might find, for example, that one aspect of your research is relevant to a much wider, more general audience. In this case, you might consider offering a small article to a national paper or a magazine. You might find an internet journal which, although not peer-reviewed, could be a useful platform for some of your research (although read our warnings about internet publication before you take the plunge). There may be an in-house publication at your university or other place of work, or a journal for your professional field, where a short article of more general interest could be well placed.

A word of warning here. Some journal editors endeavour to protect their interests by asking you to confirm that you are not offering your article to several journals at once, and that the material has not already been published elsewhere. This does not preclude the possibility of you using some of the same material in another article which takes a different slant and is submitted elsewhere, but you will need to be honest about what you are doing and, if this issue arises, tactical about how and where you offer your material in the first instance.

We are not suggesting here that you spend inordinate amounts of time in writing for publications which are outside your target area, but an article of the type mentioned above need not be as time consuming as a specialist journal article. It may help you in your networking and, as importantly, it will keep your brain in 'writing mode' whilst you await a decision on the journal article you have just submitted.

The pleasure here lies in the fact that you can be as eclectic as you like in your choice of publication. The article you write in this context is not going to be the mainstay of your publication campaign, but rather an interesting, and possibly useful, exercise in itself. If, for example, your research might have some bearing on current news events, you could consider a one-off article for a newspaper. If, on the other hand, you can see the relevance of your research to a niche group of readers other than academics, a series of short articles for a magazine would be a good idea. A colleague of ours has been working for several years on the issue of electoral reform throughout the world. It was a nice stroke of serendipity for him that electoral reform in the UK voting system happened to become, a little unexpectedly, a hot political topic. This gave him the perfect opportunity to showcase his research in a variety of publications, and to produce a popular book on electoral reform, in addition to working on his academic text on the subject.

EXERCISE

Give the possibility some thought, and record here a list of publications for which you could produce articles, but which are outside your usual publication targets:

1

2

3

4

Ideas are what make you a scholar

As well as considering new outlets for your work, you will also need to generate new ideas, so that you keep your creative levels high and feel inspired to work towards your next journal article. You can only go so far with this by yourself as most of us need some input to spur us on to the next great thought. Here are some ideas that might help:

1 Review your teaching materials, if you have some, and consider if there is anything new that you can bring to them.
2 Offer to speak to colleagues about your latest research ideas. This need not be in a formal research seminar. A gathering of interested colleagues over lunch will serve a similar purpose and might put less pressure on you.
3 Attend some research seminars, either in your own field or another area of interest. You do not have to prepare a paper or speak up, but listening to good ideas is both inspiring and useful, as you often hear a tangential idea that will help you to move on with your own work.
4 Give a paper at a conference. Conferences happily accept papers on 'works in progress' rather than anything approaching a finished piece of research and these can be vital in guiding you forwards.
5 If you do not yet feel ready to prepare a paper in a new area of your research, it is still a good idea to attend a conference, or to take a look at recent conference proceedings (either in hard copy or online), both to keep you up to date with recent developments in your area and, crucially, to give you an insight into how your peers are presenting their research findings.

Writing is what you do

It is easy to feel stagnant once you have sent off an article to a journal. Of course there will be plenty for you to do, both with your research and your other academic activities, but you have just written an article, polished it and amended it (perhaps many times) so you might feel now that you would really rather not write anything else for a while. Try to avoid this temptation if you can. By writing something, anything, you are reminding yourself that you have something to say which is worthwhile, you are keeping in the rhythm of writing, and you will be better prepared to respond to reviews and editors' comments. Writing is a bit like going to the gym or practising an instrument regularly. It is never without effort, it takes a bit of planning to find the time and your rhythm, but if you do it often enough, it becomes part of who you are and so is far easier to do.

7

WORKING WITH EDITORS AND REVIEWERS

CHAPTER OVERVIEW

This chapter will be especially helpful if:

- You have never before submitted an article.
- You are unsure about the process of moving an article from the writing stage to publication.
- Your article is nearly complete and you are tempted to send it off in its current form in the hope that someone will like it and be prepared to polish it with you.
- You dread receiving feedback on your article, worried that you will not understand what is being suggested or that it will shatter your confidence.
- You think that writing a superb article is the end of the creative process.

You will have to dispel two misconceptions about editors (and reviewers) if your journey towards a published article is to run smoothly. The first is that all you have to do is to produce an outstanding article and they will be so grateful for your brilliance that they will publish it quickly and without query or comment. The second is that they are awkward individuals whose greatest pleasure in life is to make the lives of scholars difficult. Neither of these is true, but such misconceptions come about because the relationship between editors, reviewers and writers is a delicate one which requires some nurturing. The culture of journals naturally differs from one to the next. Some editors will be able to be more accommodating to authors than others, so the amount of help you can expect in honing your article will vary. As you have no way to know in advance the culture of your chosen journal, it is best to err on the side of caution and produce the best possible product in the first instance. The role of editors is to publish the best possible article, one which will be of interest to their readers and will reflect well on your work. Your ambition is the same, of course, but it can take a little while for the relationship to develop, so in the meantime…

FIRST IMPRESSIONS REALLY DO COUNT

You will develop a creative, professional relationship with an editor, editorial panel, reviewers, technical editors and proof-readers, and this relationship might, ultimately, span decades as you continue to produce articles relevant to a particular journal during the course of your career. However, as with any relationship, the first stages are crucial. As the relationship develops, all of the qualities mentioned below will be important in varying degrees at different times in the publication process, but the first impression can only be made once, so you have to get it right. The content of the article, the hypothesis with which you are working and the evidence you can produce are the crux of your submission, of course. You might be asked to make some changes to the content at some stage, so as to make your points crystal clear, or to add weight to your argument, and this will not be a problem; indeed, it is part of the normal process of working towards publication. What is likely to be a problem, and one which you should avoid at all costs, is an article which is submitted in anticipation of huge amounts of sympathetic reading and rereading, with an editor having to work through your writing to see whether there is a publishable piece of research somehow embedded within it.

The advice we offer throughout this guide is designed to help you to produce your article in a clear and precise way, with a firm hypothesis, well crafted and supported by relevant evidence, so do not lose your nerve. Resist the temptation to put in 'stray thoughts' in the hope that an editor will see them and realise that you have plenty more to say if only you had the space. Ruthlessly weed out any evidence which, whilst interesting to you, has little value in the context of the article. Avoid including 'notes to the editor' in the article, in the form of insertions of ideas of what the article might become, if you worked on it together a little more.

It would be naïve to assume that editors have the time, or indeed the inclination, to read through article submissions repeatedly in the hope of finding something inspiring. Your job is to ensure that you grab the attention of the reader from the outset, and hold it in a focused and productive way. When you have worked through the stages outlined in this guide you will have a finished article, and you will no doubt have asked others for their advice on its content and layout. In the final stages you will call upon friends or colleagues to proofread it for you. You may well put it to one side for a week or so once it is complete, so that you can come back to it afresh and double check that there are no glaring errors which have been overlooked. All of this is to the good, naturally, but you might also consider one last check. Find a colleague, ideally someone with plenty of experience in either writing articles or working on an editorial board, and ask that colleague to submit your article to a 'confidence test'. Does it stand up as a confident piece of academic output, rather than a work that is begging for an understanding editor to realise the kernel of a good idea and work with you to make it publishable? At first reading, does it give the impression of a self-assured researcher who is able to sustain a convincing argument, within a strict word count, and in a style which is both engaging and precise? This seems like a lot to ask of your article, we know, but it is what you need to achieve in order to make the perfect first impression.

Editors and reviewers want to receive and disseminate the best possible articles. Of course they do, but they also need their writers to pay attention to, and respect, the creative relationship that achieves this, and the onus is on you to make it work even beyond that crucial first impression. As this is sometimes overlooked by writers, to their detriment, we are offering in this chapter a breakdown of what, in our experience, editors really want from their scholars.

PATIENCE

It might seem at times as if your article has become the centre of your life. You woke up thinking about it, perhaps worked late into the night to complete it, and now, finally, you have sent it off on its journey towards publication. You might get confirmation of receipt from a journal, but then nothing happens for ages. It feels as if your writing has disappeared into an academic wilderness and that nobody is taking the slightest notice of it, and this is hugely frustrating if you are waiting impatiently for a response.

Patience is essential, at this and every other stage of the process. It may be that the article sits for some time on the desk of a hard-pressed editor, but this is inevitable. It may be that you are told that the article is going out to review, but this is very likely to mean that it sits on the desks of busy academics for some weeks. These are not delays over which you have any control, but you can control your response. If you have not had an acknowledgement of receipt after several weeks, it is reasonable to make contact just to make sure that the article did actually arrive with the journal. After that, you must resolutely do nothing. You will not speed up the process by querying it, and you have plenty of others things to be doing. Every minute you spend worrying about it is a minute that could more usefully be spent elsewhere and if you keep pestering an editor you run the risk of souring the relationship even before your article is accepted.

Once your article is accepted you are still likely to face delays as you respond to reviewers' comments and wait to hear back from the editor. Articles just do take an inordinately long time to move from your computer to the printed pages of a journal, but the more patience you can muster, the more productive the process will be.

CERTAINTY

Editors need to feel confident about the provenance of any article they publish. They might insist that the article you submit is not offered for publication elsewhere whilst they consider whether or not to accept it. If the article has been disseminated in another form elsewhere, they will want to know. So, for example, if you have adapted a conference paper that has already been disseminated as a part of published conference proceedings, this will be relevant. Similarly, if you have used (or intend to use) a large part of the material in a book chapter, they will need to know. If you have already 'tried out' the article in the online environment somewhere, you need to make this clear.

This is about editors having confidence that what they print is fresh, engaging and at the forefront of their field. It is not about trying to trip you up or rejecting your article out of hand. In many cases this will be your first foray into the public domain with the material and so this aspect of publication will not be a problem, but you still need to be clear that this is the case, and abide by what you have said for however long it takes for the article to be considered by your chosen journal.

CLARITY

In the same way that you are effectively selling your ideas to readers within your article, you are now trying to catch the attention of an editor in order to 'sell' the article into a journal. A successful sale depends upon a good, clear sales pitch and, in the case of an article, this is your abstract. In Chapter 5 we discussed how to write an effective abstract, but before you send off your article, make one final check of your abstract and any keywords you have highlighted. They need to give a clear indication of what your article contains, but they need also to make the reader – and in the first place the editor – want to read the full article.

As the article progresses, it requires a sound structure. If you have followed our advice on planning and getting started, you will have this already. Planning helps to make your structure clear to you before you begin to write: now you need to ensure that it is clear to everyone else. In Chapter 3 we talked about the overall structure of your article, and in Chapter 5 we offered advice on how to 'signpost' within your writing, and you need to make sure, in your final checks on the article, that you have done both of these things. Ideally ask a colleague or friend to read through the article with only these objectives in mind. Does the structure of your article make sense, and have you signposted well enough to make this clear? It will not take you long to alter the article if a little more work is needed in this area, and you will then be offering editors the clarity which they need.

ATTENTION TO DETAIL

You need to send the editor of your chosen journal a 'clean' copy of your article. That is, an article without any typing errors or other peculiarities, which needs to be the 'finished' product, as far as you can call it finished at this stage in the process. You may find this instruction surprising, and respond by thinking 'well, obviously I am going to submit a polished and complete article', but many articles find their way to editors in what appears to be an 'advance draft' form, with mistakes left uncorrected and marginal notes still apparent. You do not want to appear arrogant, but you do want to inspire confidence, and marginal queries and comments do not give this impression, neither do obvious errors which have gone unnoticed by the writer.

Funnily enough, this is not really about proof-reading. Your article will be perused by reviewers and at least one editor, and will be proof-read several times at a later stage, by you and others. It is about showing that you value the article, that you are prepared to make the effort to submit a clean copy and that you respect your chosen journal enough to offer a beautifully produced article.

A CLEAR OBJECTIVE

This again goes back to the planning stage of your article. Your article will be well planned and, having had it checked by a supporter, you can be sure that it has a logical structure which is easy to follow, but have you made your objective clear? Why did you want to write the article in the first place? What do you hope to achieve? What would you like the reader to do with the information you are offering? What sort of reaction are you expecting? Again, we realise that this might seem obvious, but scholars can get so immersed in the detail of their research that they forget to take this overview, and sometimes they lose sight of the need for an objective even before they begin to write. This is not a difficult task, but it is worth checking before you submit that you have offered both the editor and the reader a clear objective.

TARGETED WRITING

From the outset of this guide we have stressed the need to target a specific readership for your article, and this will have involved considering several publications and then immersing yourself in the writing style of a particular journal before you came to write. This process must continue right up until the point of submission. An editor will be looking for articles which seem to 'fit', in terms of writing style, format and structure, research stance and material. If you fail to achieve this fit, you will make it extremely hard for an editor to see why your article is perfect for your chosen journal, so working to this remit of producing a sufficiently targeted article will always be to your benefit. In essence, the article must fit the brief of the journal, not vice versa.

The sections above all stress the practicalities of producing your article. You will also need to foster some key personal qualities:

RELIABILITY

To quell any doubts you might have about this aspect of journal production: the instructions you are given are not intended to be unnecessarily onerous, nor are they produced at the whim of a cantankerous editorial team. Editors are incredibly busy and the smooth flow of production relies heavily upon everyone playing their part with equal dedication. You will have researched your chosen journal and so will know what is expected of you. If you are not sure, check. If you are asked to produce an article in twelve-point font, sans serif and with double spacing, then do exactly that.

At every stage of the publication process you will need to follow every instruction meticulously, but in this first stage, that of submitting your article, failing to follow instructions can have one of several dire effects. It might seem that you have little interest in this particular journal, and that you are simply touting your article around the marketplace in the hope of becoming published. You might come across as arrogant, concerned more with your brilliant article than with the needs of the journal. You might seem half-hearted, with little real ambition to become a published scholar. Disastrous effects indeed, and entirely avoidable if you simply follow the instructions you are given, without question or deviation.

COMMUNICATION

Although we have urged you to have patience as you await a response to your article, you should not expect the same level of patience from members of the journal's editorial team. They are not going to be unreasonable, but they are likely to come up with urgent queries and need answers quickly. They also need reassurance that you will be available whenever you are needed.

To some extent the challenge of communication between scholars and journals has been greatly reduced by the use of email, as long as you answer their emails as quickly as you reasonably can. If your article has been submitted to a journal which is published in a country in a significantly different time zone from your home country, email may be the only effective form of communication between you, and this can lend an even greater sense of urgency to the emails you receive.

As you keep up regular communication with the journal, it makes sense to consider the production process through which your article will be passing. There will be well defined phases in this process, and you will be made aware of these by your journal, but make sure that the editorial team is made aware of any unavoidable gaps in your working schedule, such as holidays. If you receive an email and you cannot get to it right away, then let them know. No editor is likely to object if you reply and explain that you are about to leave for a three-day conference abroad and you will reply on your return, but an unexplained gap in communication at a critical point is bound to cause some level of anxiety. Again, this is all about fostering an excellent creative relationship with your editor.

COMMITMENT

It can be unexpectedly hard work to see an article through from the writing phase to publication. There may well be times when you are sick of the sight of it. At other times you might become worried that it is changing too much as reviewers and your editor try to guide it towards publication. Some months after you wrote it you will still be returning to it to answer queries and, perhaps, make changes, and this can be gruelling. Added to all of this, you are working to the journal's timetable rather than your own, and so emails will arrive at the most inconvenient moments.

You have to summon up your reserves of commitment as you go through the process, and the best way we have found to do this is to look back to earlier stages. We recall our excitement when we first thought of the idea for the article, and our elation when it was accepted. We also remember, with some gratitude, that there is no suspense involved at this point. We are not asking anyone to approve of or accept the article for publication, but are simply working as part of a team so as to make it the best possible article for publication. This is not an infallible way to keep yourself from flagging, but it does help to get you in the right frame of mind to keep up your commitment to the process.

RESILIENCE

Receiving constructive criticism about an article which you have submitted is an oddly artificial situation, and it is perhaps for this reason that writers sometimes react more negatively to it than one might expect. If you were to give a paper or presentation in a research seminar, surrounded by six or so of your fellow scholars, you would find the process challenging, but also enlightening. If anyone questioned the structure of your paper, or the way in which you had described your methodology, you would be eager to explain why you did things as you did, but you would also be happy to accept that the paper is not perfect. Any criticism of the paper, even forthright criticism, would be taken in the way that it was meant, and you would be content to make changes in the light of the comments you receive. There are several reasons for this. You are amongst your peers, and trust their input. You see your paper as a work in progress, one which is open to change and development. Most importantly, you can see your critics face to face and so feel comfortable with the situation.

Receiving anonymous criticism from a distance is a far less comfortable situation. You have worked hard on your article and submitted it in the belief that it is, as near as anything can be, the finished product. You then receive, some time later, a series of reviewers' comments which, unless you are feeling very robust, can quickly seem like nothing more than a list of critical and unhelpful comments. You are, of course, a little nervous and you will feel vulnerable. If you are very busy when the comments arrive, you might also feel that this is just one more pressure on you.

The secret to working well with reviewers, and being able to take on board any criticism of your article, is to take an overview of the situation by remembering three key points.

THE AIM OF THE REVIEWERS

Reviewers have a clear task to accomplish: either to reject the article for that particular publication (see Chapter 8 for more on this) or to offer constructive criticism so as to make it the best possible article before it goes to print. Being sent an article for review tends to bring with it an implied requirement to make some criticism, so you will need to become adept at reading reviews in a positive light. A minor suggestion is not going to cause you a problem at all, and you will be able to see that the small change you might make in response will improve your article's structure or strengthen your overall argument.

Where reviewers' comments become more burdensome is when major changes are suggested. The first thing to do is to take a step back. Is the suggested change really major, or are you simply responding negatively to any criticism at all? If it is a major change, follow the suggestions offered later in this chapter to help you to respond positively.

THEY ARE EXPERTS IN YOUR FIELD

Although you will (with very few exceptions) receive anonymous criticism on your article, you can be sure that your chosen journal will have sent it out to review amongst experts in your field. After all, there would be no point in doing anything else. Your role in this is therefore to imagine that the comments are coming from your supervisor, or a panel of academics at a research review meeting. This will help you to respond positively, with an acceptance that you are not, yet, the leading expert in your field nor, probably, do you have a wealth of publication experience to draw upon. The benefit to you of receiving reviewers' comments is huge. Remember that their names will not be on the finished article. However much their comments improve it, your name will attach to those improvements and they are doing you an enormous scholarly favour here.

THEY ARE NOT EXPERTS IN YOUR ARTICLE

Having said all of that, you will also need to recognise that this remains your article. Reviewers, on occasion, cannot resist trying to rewrite the article from a distance, so that it reflects more closely the way that they would choose to write it. There are also times when an article goes out to review with an expert who simply disagrees with the whole premise of the article, and so is unlikely to say anything positive about it. If your editorial team have not rejected the article in the light of reviewers' comments, then you are in a position to accept many of the suggested changes (and you will want to do this, because they make sense to you) and to reject some suggestions (because you can give good reasons why they would not improve the article or would distort your argument too greatly).

This is a delicate balance to achieve: responding positively to criticism and yet not being so deferential as to make changes which will, in your view, mar your article. You need a finished product of which you are proud, and which serves the purposes you set out to achieve. There are ways to approach this situation which we have found helpful over the years:

- We never open the letter or email attachment which contains reviewers' comments until we can make time to sit down and thoroughly peruse the documents without interruption. This may mean that they sit, unread, for a couple of days, but this is better than glancing at them in a rush. If you do this, you will find that, in the time it takes before you can look at them properly, all you can remember are what you took to be the negative comments.

- For our joint authored projects we take a similar approach in our discussions. When we have both read the reviewers' comments on our book proposals, we try to avoid responding to each other in corridors as we rush from one place to the next. Instead, we set up a meeting so that we have enough time to talk them through properly.
- We remind ourselves that this is meant to be *constructive* criticism. If one reviewer appears to have taken against a project altogether, we will leave those comments until last in our consideration, so that we can view them in a more balanced way in the light of the other comments we have received.
- It will have been some time since we looked at the work which was submitted (in the case of our joint authored projects, this will usually be a book proposal or sample chapter). We print off a copy of the work, skim read it and make a few marginal notes on it wherever we can see, with hindsight, that it could be improved. This is not because we are necessarily going to make those changes, but rather it is a way for us to 'break up' the text a little, so that we are reminded that this is a work in progress, which will develop further in the light of reviewers' comments, rather than a closed, finished piece of writing.
- When we are working as co-authors we are in the lucky position of being able to talk to each other about reviewers' comments. You need to put yourself in a similar position. Once you have taken time to consider the comments, and written some notes in response, take them to your supervisor or mentor for a second opinion. The discussion that you have is likely to endorse some of your responses, and help to validate some of the comments which you found more difficult to take. If you do not agree entirely with a reviewer's viewpoint on one aspect of the article, this discussion will help shape your response to the editorial team.
- This is not about 'you' versus 'them'. It is not a battle of opinions, but it does make sense for you to gauge opinion on some of the comments. The majority of the suggestions made will not cause you any great angst, and you will be happy to make the changes implied by those comments. If you feel that a few of the comments are not going to improve your article, or may distort your central message, it makes sense to ask colleagues and other experts in your field. However, this cannot become farcical. You would be doing yourself a disservice if you spent weeks sending out a few comments to everyone in your field, chorusing your distress at receiving them and asking for support. Not only is this unproductive, you also risk sending the message out to the very reviewer who made the comment in the first place.
- Constructive criticism requires a constructive response, so be clear. Give a full response to the entire set of comments to the editorial team of your journal, explaining both why you are happy to accept some of the suggestions and why, if necessary, you are reluctant to make changes in response to other suggestions. In reality, most of us would make changes in response to the vast majority of the comments made.
- It is a case here also of responding in the right tone. An email to the editorial team in which you are clearly upset by any criticism or, worse still, angry at

the very thought that you might have to make changes, puts the team in an awkward position and will put a strain on the creative process as you move forward. So, be clear and precise about what you plan to do as a result of reviewers' comments, but be positive and accepting of criticism. It is not always easy to achieve, but it is the best way to respond.

We have focused in this chapter on the challenges you will face in working with editors and reviewers, but we would not want you to overlook the fact that this is intended to be a positive relationship. It is pleasing to work as part of a team, knowing that you are all aiming for the same goal, that of producing an article of which you will all be proud. Looking back, we realise that some of 'our' best ideas have actually had their genesis in the comments of editors or reviewers. We may have developed them, and made them our own, but we are pleased that, when it comes to publication, you are always part of a creative team.

USEFUL WEBSITES

www.vitae.ac.uk/researchers
www.ukcge.ac.uk

8

RECOVERING FROM REJECTION

CHAPTER OVERVIEW

This chapter will be especially helpful if:

- An article you have submitted was not accepted by a journal and you are not sure why this happened.
- You are worried about how to cope with rejection. You know that you struggle to accept constructive criticism of your work.
- You would like to take a positive approach to the possibility of rejection.
- Fear of rejection is causing you to delay submitting an article, or putting you off the whole idea of writing an article.
- You are waiting to hear from a journal and it is playing on your mind so much that you cannot seem to focus on other things you need to be doing.

IT HAPPENS TO EVERYONE

There is no doubt that the sinking feeling you get when you are informed that your article will not be published in your chosen journal is just horrible. You will feel one (or more) of many things. Shock perhaps, if you were convinced that it would be accepted. This is a good emotion under the circumstances, in that it means that you absolutely believed in what you were writing and are convinced that it should reach a wider audience. This will lead to a positive approach to the future of the article, given time. You might feel extremely upset, and why not? You have worked hard and produced something which you feel is of real merit, and then you have exposed yourself to the chance of rejection. Feeling upset is the most natural reaction, so let it happen. If you need to, put the article to one side for a time, until you feel ready to approach it positively again. You could feel angry, which you will have to hope is short-lived, as it is probably misplaced. It is not you who has been rejected, but your article, and it has been rejected for a reason. You need to overcome any anger so that you can grasp that reason and move on.

Whilst all of these reactions are expected and can be overcome or used productively, the most common reaction – and one which it is totally unnecessary to feel – is embarrassment. You have already shared your thoughts with your supervisor or mentor, and perhaps with family and friends. Your fellow researchers and colleagues may know that you have submitted the article for publication, and so you dread having to say that, as you see it at the moment, you have failed in your endeavour. It is difficult to grasp that you have not actually failed at all. You have simply stumbled over one hurdle and will now move on to jump the next.

The most detrimental effect of feeling embarrassed and upset is that we inevitably tend to assume that this has not happened to everyone around us, but of course it has. All scholars would be able to tell you of the many rejections they have received, from submitting journal articles, to book proposals, to major bids for funding. It is an inherent part of a system where supply drastically outstrips demand, and it becomes far easier to bear the more you have gone through it. As we write this we are both cringing slightly, swapping stories, for the first time, about our failed attempts in the past to gain funding for much cherished projects.

The 'first time' in the sentence above is perhaps the most important phrase to notice (after all, we would rather you did not dwell on our defeats!), because it is only natural to avoid lengthy conversations about reverses in our otherwise happy careers. Scholars might moan about the difficulty of getting work published, and the tremendous pressure on us all to publish regularly despite this, but we would hesitate to tell even our closest colleagues about just how awful we felt when things went wrong, even though we knew at the time that these things really do happen to everyone at one time or another.

It is for this reason that, as soon as you can manage it, you need to tell people about the rejection, because it is only by telling your tale that you will encourage people to share their experiences. There is nothing like your supervisor reeling off a list of personal horror stories to make you feel better.

TELLING PEOPLE

It is possible to make telling people about the rejection into a positive experience which will help you to overcome your present feelings and move you forward in your planning, but this must be done in different ways if you are to get the most helpful response.

Your family

Of course your family will be upset if you are upset, but remember that they may have little real idea about how much this means to you (at the moment), so prepare carefully. You might want to blurt out that your article (not you) has been rejected, but then be as generous as you can. Take time to explain why you are upset, especially if you have not discussed the article in much detail before, and allow them time to appreciate why you feel bad about it. Then, when they are at a suitable pitch of sympathetic misery, use that sympathy to propel yourself forward by explaining to them how you intend to move forward from the disappointment.

Your colleagues

If you are working professionally whilst undertaking your research, you may be in a position where your work colleagues are all aware of the article and its submission. You might even be relying on its publication as part of your bid for promotion. You will need to think carefully about whom to tell. You might tell nobody, on the basis that you can resubmit the article elsewhere and so only have a good news story to tell later on. If you do tell people (and this could gain you useful support), then have the entire picture ready in your mind. There is little to be gained from simply declaring that your article has been rejected. How would colleagues know how to respond? Instead, understand why the article was rejected so that you can give a fuller picture ('My article was rejected because … and so I am going to …). That way your colleagues can talk to you enthusiastically about your plans rather than simply commiserating. Your boss will also see your response as positive, rather than taking away a wholly negative image of the situation.

Your fellow scholars

We like to think of academia as a collegiate idyll, one in which scholars work together, spurred on by intellectual curiosity and determination, in order to achieve the best work possible. For the most part, it is exactly that (which is why it is such a pleasure to work within it) but we would be naïve to ignore the other side of the idyll. It is also a space in which everyone is striving to achieve individually, if not in direct competition with colleagues, then at least with an awareness that only the very best succeed. As the supply of journal articles outstrips demand, you will need to bear in mind that not all of your immediate colleagues will react to your rejection as you might reasonably expect. If fellow scholars in your immediate circle are also awaiting news on journal articles which they have submitted, they may be loath to discuss the subject at all. If they have just had an article accepted, they may be so delighted as to find it difficult to sympathise with your situation. If they are in the same position as you, they may launch into a tirade of despair which does nothing to make you feel more positive. There is nothing you can do about any of these factors, except to be aware of them when you come to tell people of your disappointment.

Your supervisor or mentor

Your supervisor or mentor will, of course, be sympathetic if your article is rejected, and will be keen to explain to you that this is an unavoidable part of the life of a scholar. However, he or she is also likely to be circumspect, concerned not to upset you or say the wrong thing, so you may have to take the lead here. The best way to do this is to consider the comments you have received from the journal and work out an initial response. In this way you can tell your supervisor or mentor that the article has been rejected, and that you can see why this has happened (if you really can see at this stage) and that you would like to discuss how best to move forward. This does not preclude the possibility of plenty of sympathy when you have your next meeting, and this will be well meant and welcome, but it does reassure everyone involved that you are not going to crumble under the weight of one rejection.

Having considered how best you might spread the news of your disappointment in such a way that you receive the most productive response from all of those around you, we now want to consider with you ways in which you might decrease your feelings of disappointment and increase your chances of moving forward swiftly and positively.

PREPARE FOR REJECTION

This may seem, at first glance, to be a negative stance to take even before you have had an article rejected, but actually it is a positive action to take as it ensures that you will cope with rejection, should it come, far better than if you just sat back and wished for success. In Chapter 6 we offered ideas as to what you might do to keep up your momentum once you had completed an article, and the same principles work well in this situation. If you have plenty of productive activity planned whilst your article is being considered, it makes it far easier to continue with this if you receive a rejection. If you have been lacking focus because you are eagerly awaiting a response, it can be difficult to get your motivation back if the article is not accepted by your chosen journal. There are several practical steps you can take to help prepare early.

Decide whom to tell

We have considered in this chapter the possible responses you might expect as you let people know that your article has been rejected. As you submit it, you might target in your mind the first person you will tell: someone who will be hugely sympathetic and help to keep your spirits up.

Have a specific task ready for that moment

Choose an achievable, satisfying task to turn to on the day that you receive the rejection letter. Not only will this make you feel better, but it will also ensure that you do not waste too much of your precious time focusing only on the rejection to the detriment of all the others things you need to get done.

Have a back-up plan for the article

How you feel about your article if it is rejected by your chosen journal will depend on the sort of person you are. You might want to lock it in a drawer and ignore it; you might want to revise it for resubmission immediately. Both of these responses are valid and neither will put you at a disadvantage, as long as you have a plan in advance. If it is to be consigned to a drawer, promise yourself that it will only be for a week or two; if you want to work on it straight away, make sure that you do this with the advice of your mentor or supervisor. Ignoring it forever is a waste of a good article; ripping it to pieces and reassembling it without any great thought is not going to help your chances in resubmission.

Use the article material whilst you wait

You were obviously pleased with the article when you submitted it, but it then takes on a transient life in your mind, as you respond emotionally to the waiting. Some days you will remember it as a thing of perfection. On others you will wonder why you submitted it at all. Neither of these responses is based in reality, of course. You need to remind yourself of the quality of your article, whilst remaining aware that, as with any human endeavour, it has areas which could be open to improvement. A good way to do this is to use the material. It will be some time before you hear whether it has been accepted, so if you can use some of the material for your teaching, or garner some of the arguments for a research seminar, this will help to keep you anchored in the reality of the article and will ensure that your response to rejection is realistic and positive.

Prepare other articles

Preparing an article for submission can be mentally exhausting, and few of us feel inspired to write a brand new article the moment we have submitted. However, you can take advantage of the fact that your mind is working in 'article mode' and begin to plan your next several articles (see Chapter 6). You might not feel like writing, but sketching out some ideas and making an out-line plan are both useful and productive distractions from your submitted article, and you might find that you begin to write some draft sections. We have both found that the week or so after a disappointment can be an extremely fruitful time to move on to other projects in this way.

See it as a deferment of publication

This may literally be the case, as sometimes an apparent rejection can actually be just a 'revise and resubmit it' instruction. In other cases, however, this is not so. The reviewers' remarks might make it seem highly unlikely that your chosen journal would ever accept the article and this can leave you feeling despondent. However, it is worth us reiterating here that you will face many setbacks in your life as a scholar, and persistency really does pay off. If you can see a rejection as a deferment, it is far easier to begin to consider what you might do next with the article and this will depend on the reviewers' comments, which we will consider next.

USE THE REVIEWS

The reviewers of your article undertook their task with a view to seeing whether the article was suitable for your chosen journal, but of course they are also working to your benefit. The feedback you get with a rejection will be crucial as you consider what to do next. This form of feedback is unusual in that you will not know the identity of your reviewers and so, unlike most academic feedback, you will not be in a position to know more about their views than what has been written down for you. This means that you have to become a scholarly detective, reading not only what is written, but also between the lines to learn as much as possible about their views on the article.

This 'between the lines' aspect of discerning reviewers' comments is where paranoia can easily creep in. A reviewer makes a minor comment about a little awkwardness of style in a couple of places and you instantly want to completely rewrite the article. One negative comment on the research, however slight, can lead you straight to the matches to destroy the whole article. That is why you need help and advice at this stage. In the first instance you will want to consider the comments in peace and quiet and perhaps mull over them for a while, but then *always* make sure that you get a second opinion. Remember that more experienced scholars will not only have faced a similar situation, but they also may have been reviewers for journals themselves, and so will be in an excellent position to keep you on the right track as you review the comments.

Understanding in detail why your article has been rejected is clearly going to be a major step in moving forward. It is worth noting here that your article might be rejected without much review, although this is unlikely to happen if you have researched your chosen journal thoroughly. This is actually the easiest type of rejection to handle. Although you will be immensely frustrated to have the article rejected, if this happens because you have simply missed your target (for example, if the journal is not intending to cover this area of your field in the future) or because you have not fitted your article to general requirements (for example, it is twice as long as it should be) then you at least have the reassurance of knowing that you chose the wrong journal, rather than there being any intrinsic problem with the article.

If you are given detailed feedback (and one should always hope for detailed feedback, rather than frustratingly vague, general comments), then you are in a position to consider making changes to the article. You will need to check first whether the journal would be prepared to consider a revised version of the article; if not, you might still need to make changes before submitting it elsewhere, but your response to the reviews may be different. Comments which seem to you (and your advisors) to relate only to publication in that particular journal are more easily put to one side if this is no longer your target publication.

Whilst reviewers all have their own style in producing feedback, we offer you here some guidelines as to the type of feedback you might expect to see, and make suggestions as to how you can most usefully respond. Remember that your article will not necessarily have been rejected for just one of these failings, so you will need to read the comments in conjunction with each other. It is also unlikely that an article would be *accepted* with no constructive criticism at all, so the guidelines offered here will also be of use to you if your article is accepted for publication.

Style

Minor problems of style can be addressed relatively easily as an article journeys towards print. However, if all of the reviewers of your rejected article comment unfavourably on your writing style you must take this seriously. In a competitive field, not being able to write fluently and persuasively is going to be a significant hurdle for you. The advice we offer in Chapter 5 will help to eliminate some common problems, but you will need to steel yourself to do far more if your poor writing style is getting in the way of your success. This is not necessarily a bad thing: it may be just the hint you need to get some help with your writing, a move which is probably long overdue.

Topic

This can be an unnerving comment to receive from a reviewer. You have researched your chosen journal and selected the topic for your article carefully, so how could you possibly have got it so wrong? The answer might be nothing to do with your efforts, of course, if the editorial team has decided to change the focus of the journal. However, if there is no obvious reason outside your control as to why this has come up as a comment, go back and consider exactly what is being said. Is it really the entire topic which is being dismissed as unsuitable for that publication, or merely one part of it? Are the reviewers saying that the topic is too broad for a single article? Or perhaps they are suggesting that you have dwelt too much on ground which has been covered before, rather than focusing on the more ground-breaking aspects of your research? It is only by discovering these nuances in response that you can decide how much, or how little, of the article needs to be reassessed.

Approach

A response which seems critical of your approach is tricky to pin down, and it is unlikely to be a true criticism of your work as such. It is more likely to be a reflection of your research into your chosen journal. Although the topics which tend to be covered in a journal are obvious, some journals favour particular approaches to the material in articles and the ways in which arguments are formed and research is conducted. If this was not obvious to you in your initial examination of your chosen journal, the comments of reviewers will prompt you to reinterrogate this aspect of your article.

Argument

If the reviewers suggest that your argument does not hold together sufficiently, or that your argument is too weak, this might be relatively easy to correct. It is usually the case that a writer has become so engrossed in the research material that the purpose of that material, to create a persuasive and compelling argument, has been lost. The easiest way to cope with this challenge is to take a highlighter pen to your article and indicate each point at which you are stating or developing your argument. Then check through each of the highlighted sentences and see whether, when read in isolation in this way, they do hang together as a linear argument. If, on reflection, it becomes clear to you that you have not produced a convincing argument, some rewriting will be necessary. The key here is to go back to your original plan, considering how and where you can strengthen your argument and, if you feel it will take some significant additional writing, identifying which material in your plan you can safely abandon in order to keep to your word count.

Research material

If you are told that you have not carried out sufficient research to support your argument this is, on the face of it, a fairly dismal comment. However, it is not necessarily a true reflection of the situation as you know it to be. Two factors are likely to be at play here. Either you became so caught up in the rhetoric of the argument that you sliced away too much of the research material which supported it, or your enthusiasm has led you to make sweeping statements which you are not yet in a position to back up. Both of these positions can be remedied if you take a step back. If your problem is the former, indicate on your article with two different coloured pens which sections contain your research material and which contain principally argument. You will see instantly how the proportions are working. You can then précis down the language of the argument sections in order to leave adequate space to introduce more research material. This might sound onerous, but it can actually be quite a pleasurable experience: you are simultaneously honing your writing skills and improving the balance of your article.

If your problem is the latter, be grateful to the reviewers: they have just saved you from disaster. To make unsubstantiated claims is unforgivable in the academic world, so be ruthless. Again using a highlighter pen, identify and then firmly cut out any claims you have made which have not been supported by material *in the article*. There is no benefit to you telling yourself that you are sure you are right and can prove it from work you have done elsewhere. An article must stand alone on its merits and all of its claims must be supported by the work within it. In some cases you will simply have overlooked the need to refer in enough detail to the work of others in making your claims, but elsewhere you are likely to have to simply remove a claim, however painful this may be, so that the article is an integral entity in and of itself. The claims you delete will not be wasted: they are about to form the basis of your next article.

Before our checklist on types of feedback we mentioned that you are in a position to 'consider' making changes to your article. This is an important point. You are in a position to reject the opinion of the reviewers, but only with the utmost caution. You can see from some of the comments in the checklist that the reviewers might, on occasion, be rejecting an article for that particular journal but not necessarily rejecting it as an article in itself, and you need to bear this in mind. As you work through the comments with your supervisor, mentor or other colleagues, make notes on which of the comments seem to you all to be justified in their entirety, and which seem to relate only to your chosen journal and so may not be relevant in terms of resubmission elsewhere, and which you feel, between you, can safely be taken on only in part. Of course you will not want to reject out-of-hand comments which have been made by leading experts in the field, but you need to keep in the back of your mind the fact that this is still your article, and you must be able to resubmit any revised version happy in the knowledge that it is improved, but still essentially an article which reflects your research in a way that sits happily with you.

MAKE A PLAN OF ACTION

Scholars are usually happiest when they have a clear idea of what they hope to achieve. We are all happy to work in freefall for short periods of time. Our research often dictates that we do this, but before long we like to bring order to chaos, and this is what you will need to do now. By working through the guidance in this chapter you will, we hope, have a clear idea of why your article was rejected. You are now in a position to make a clear plan of action, and you are going to need this if you are not to lose your way. You will need to decide which chapter in this book to turn to first in your reworking of the piece and your plan of action must include a firm timescale so that you do not lose your sense of purpose as you return to the article.

We are, all of us, scholars because we feel passionate about our subject area and feel that our research is not just valuable in itself, but also reveals new insights which we want to share with others. The downside to this way of seeing the world is that we are bitterly disappointed if an article is rejected. The upside is that, once we understand why it happened and can see a clear way forward, that passion swiftly reasserts itself and what seems at first sight to be nothing more than a rejection becomes an opportunity to offer an even better insight into our work.

9

INTELLECTUAL PROPERTY RIGHTS

CHAPTER OVERVIEW

This chapter will be especially helpful if:

- You have never given much thought to intellectual property rights.
- Offering your research to a wide audience makes you anxious.
- The competing claims to intellectual property are confusing you.
- You want the best outlet for your work, without impeding your rights.
- You want to share credit for parts of your work, but are not sure how to do this appropriately, protecting the rights of all concerned.
- You have been asked to contribute to an article and are not sure how this affects your rights.
- You want to use the internet to best advantage.

AN OVERVIEW

In thinking about this chapter we were reminded of the great scientist Sir Isaac Newton. As a man of science and member of the Royal Society, he did what any academic would do: he shared his ideas for the greater good and contributed hugely to advances in his field. However, as an alchemist he was far less giving. Like his fellow alchemists, he wrapped his hypotheses and methodology in a disguise of verse and allegory which was fairly impenetrable to his contemporaries and even more difficult to access by scholars today. Of course, he and his colleagues failed in their alchemical goal because what they were trying to achieve seems impossible (we say 'seems' because it would be foolhardy to assume that anything is impossible within academia), but they failed far more profoundly as scholars because they simply refused to share their knowledge. Thus, failed experiments were repeated, doomed hypotheses were reintroduced numerous times, and nobody was willing to work together with others in order to advance the field.

There is an element of this approach in some areas of academia today: a natural reluctance to share an idea until you have proved its merit to yourself, a wariness of 'giving away' your hypothesis in case someone else can develop a methodology to prove it before you, or in case you look less clever than you had hoped. The challenge here lies in understanding the mechanics of academia. It relies upon sharing, and you will find, as you gain more experience, that scholars are both generous in their willingness to share and painstaking in their attempts to give credit where it is due.

There are mechanisms in place to ensure that your intellectual property (often just called 'IP') is protected, and it goes without saying, perhaps, that this is an area which you need to check thoroughly in each instance before you publish, but you might like to consider here some of the competing demands upon you.

GENEROSITY VS PROTECTION

This is often the first dilemma faced by a researcher considering publication, and it is an issue which we initially addressed in Chapter 1 of this guide. You naturally want to gain credit for your work, but you will also come to see the benefits of sharing. One of the authors of this guide was reminded here of one of her earliest experiences of the importance of sharing in this way. She was working on the hypothesis that women in Early Modern England might have had some influence over the contents of their funeral sermons. This seemed like an exciting, and fairly new, hypothesis to a young postgraduate research student and she kept the idea to herself for some weeks, scouring the literature and finding out that this was a little-explored area.

It was at this point that she was asked to give one of her first conference papers, at a relatively informal gathering consisting predominantly of postgraduate students and early career researchers. On checking the delegate list it became clear that several of the delegates had an interest in a similar area, and she felt an instinctive reluctance to share her early findings, concerned that someone more advanced in research in the field might have the material in hand to pursue the thought far more speedily than she would be able to do.

It took a lengthy meeting with her supervisor to persuade her that she should present at the conference, despite her misgivings, and she gave a paper covering one rather limited area of her research into funeral sermons, relying on just the few examples she had found. To her amazement, a distinguished scholar approached her after her paper and explained that he had received funding some years previously to produce a database of funeral sermons from the period, but that he had not yet had time to carry out research on the material, and his interest was not specifically slanted to female funeral sermons, so would she like the database to advance her research? Two days later the database arrived in her email, saving her weeks, perhaps months, of research time. This was the perfect example of scholarly sharing, made poignant by the fact that, quite unexpectedly, the distinguished scholar died several months later, and his database might have been lost had she not overcome her concerns, and had he been less generous.

This example shows that sharing works, and of course we do it all the time. Ironically, whilst you might be a little anxious about giving your hypotheses and material a public airing, the very act of publication is a far better way to secure your intellectual property rights than by informal, unpublished sharing.

> Academia relies on generosity, but it will also protect you.

PRIVATE VS PUBLIC

Sometimes a reluctance to publish is less a rational concern about protecting your intellectual property rights, and more of an emotional hurdle. We discussed this in Chapter 6: the unnerving feeling that, once you make your work available to public scrutiny, you are setting yourself up to be judged by others. Of course, you are doing just this, but you are also doing so much more. You are allowing others to see your progress, to engage with you in your endeavours to support a hypothesis, and to offer their support and admiration for your achievements.

Publication can seem like a loss of ownership as you offer your material, and as importantly your analysis of that material, to a wider public. Although it may seem counter intuitive, putting forward a journal article for publication is in many ways more like staking a claim to ownership of that material and those ideas: you will be forever credited with that work and those ideas, however embryonic they are and however they are used by others in your field in the future.

This fear of exposure can be paralysing, even in experienced academics. We were once at the retirement party of a scholar who was renowned in his field. In his early career he had published numerous books and articles, but as he advanced in his career he became increasingly concerned to hoard his material, to keep new findings to himself with the idea that he would get around to publishing them at some point. It was sad to see a colleague retire, of course, but made all the more sad by the fact that we were fully aware that we were also saying goodbye to a decade or so of material gathering that was unlikely to come to fruition. That retirement party was seven years ago and he has yet to publish in retirement.

If the anxieties surrounding publication are clear, and so too are the potential benefits, you could see the writing of an article as a test as to whether you are ready to let it loose on the world. We have suggested in this guide that you do plenty of research on journals in your field, and have your target readership in mind as you write. Now we are also suggesting that you keep in mind that you are not compelled to publish any particular article. If you feel, as you might, that the material and your hypothesis are not yet mature enough for publication, you are free to move on to another area of your subject and plan an article from there, filing away your original article in its early form for a time when you will be ready to publish it. The reason we suggest taking this approach is that it is hard, in prospect, to work out which particular aspect of your research is the right one to pick for publication. It is only by going through the early stages of the process: identifying a topic, researching possible journals for publication, planning an article, that you can get a good idea of whether this is the right article, at the right time.

> Use the early stages of preparing an article as a test of whether this is the right article, at the right time. Abandoned articles can easily be picked up later, once the material and your hypothesis have matured.

ACKNOWLEDGEMENT VS CITATION

Every student, from the moment of entering university, starts to gain an awareness of the dangers of plagiarism, even unintentional plagiarism. You will know by now, as if by instinct, that you must always, always cite the work of others as you use it. However, in an article, where you are likely to be condensing fairly complex ideas and often generating rather speculative new research areas, you face another challenge. You will be relying on the experience and ideas of others, and may well include the results of research seminars, conference discussions and even casual conversations with experts. Often, these have not been published and so might not be cited in the normal way, but you must still take painstaking care to acknowledge the help of others, even if you cannot cite their published work directly. There is absolutely no advantage to missing this vital step in preparing your work for publication, and a failure to do so is not only unethical, but fraught with danger.

> Your reputation rests not only with what you produce, but also with how well you seem to respect other people's intellectual property rights.

RESEARCHER VS UNIVERSITY/EMPLOYER

It seems simple in prospect. You have developed a hypothesis, you devise the methodology and then you interpret your results and write them up. Except, of course, that it is not that simple. Your university may well have rights over your intellectual property, as might your employer. This is a complex area and one about which you must be entirely clear before you offer your work for publication. There is a series of questions to ask yourself here:

- If you intend to publish material which is the subject of a patent, is that patent held (or going to be held) in your name or is it the property of your employer and/or your university?
- If you are working on a joint project with your supervisor (in this case referred to often as the Principal Investigator), do you have permission to publish?
- Do you need to clear your article with an ethics committee, remembering that both your work area and your institution might have separate ethics committees? This might be a requirement placed upon you by your institution, your employer or your chosen journal, so make sure that you make enquiries about this aspect of publication early on in the process.
- If you have received funding for your research, does your funding body have the right to dictate what you may publish?
- If your research project is part of a university-wide endeavour, who is deciding on when and where the findings are published?
- If your employers have a commercial stake in your research, have they approved the publication?

The number of questions here is an indication of how complicated an issue this can be, but we would urge you not to be put off. You will be able to publish your findings, but you will need to factor into your plans the need to ensure that you have covered all bases with regard to intellectual property rights. Your supervisor or mentor would be the first person to approach, followed if needs be by the research and enterprise department of your academic institution, and, if you are employed outside academia, the legal/research department of your employer. It seems daunting, but even if the commercial or cash benefits of your work go entirely or principally to your institution, your career will benefit from publication.

> Consider how any division of intellectual property rights on your research might affect your journal article in the earliest stages of planning. It can take some time to gain approval, but the professional benefits should be worth the effort.

RESEARCHER VS JOURNAL

Once your article is published, the journal in which it is published will have claims on it alongside your own intellectual property rights. This will be spelled out to you clearly by your chosen journal, but as a general rule you must assume that you are not in a position to reuse the article, or sections of the article, without the express permission, in writing, of the journal. This laying of a claim by a journal may begin even before publication, as some journals ask you to guarantee upon submission that the article, or material contained within the article, is not being offered for publication elsewhere. In practical terms, a journal will not be served by restricting your access to the material, and it is common enough for articles to be reused in various guises in subsequent publications such as books, but always with an acknowledgement of the journal in which the material was first published. Debate rages at present about the desirability of the practice of reusing material in this way, but the choice will be yours as long as you have ensured that you follow the correct procedure of permission, acknowledgement and citation.

Whilst you will want to recognise the right that a journal in which you have published has on your intellectual property, there are occasions when you might have to take action to secure your reputation. We recently came across a case of a scholar who had produced an article for a journal on the subject of French history. The article was a great success, and the journal editorial board decided that it should be translated into French for publication in a sister journal in that country. The board was within its rights to make such a decision, but overlooked the possibility that, as the scholar was bilingual, she might want to undertake the translation herself. The first she knew of the decision was when she saw her article in print in the French journal, with a rudimentary mistake in the translation in the very first paragraph. Although this was little more than an irritation (the mistranslation did not spoil the meaning of the article overall), she clearly wished that she had discussed her rights in translation prior to agreeing to the publication of the article.

> Assume that your intellectual property rights will be fundamentally affected by publication, and ensure that you respect the claims of your chosen journal, whilst protecting your own reputation.

HARD COPY VS INTERNET

From an academic's perspective, the internet is both a delight and a danger. There is material to be found there on every subject under the sun, but we are well aware that, too often, that material is unverified, even on professional looking sites. We become so used to accessing the internet as a first source of information that publishing an article on it can seem like a natural progression for a researcher. Of course, your material will find its way onto the internet as your career progresses: conference proceedings may be lodged on there, and journals will usually have an online presence. As a result, this opposition between hard copy and the internet may seem like an artificial distinction, but there are key points to consider. First, let us look at the advantages:

- It can be a quick route to a form of publication.
- Your work will reach a wide ranging readership.
- Applications for funding might be enhanced if you can point to publications on the internet, especially if you have developed your own research group on the web.
- You can be more eclectic in your choice of material.
- You can usually reuse material with impunity, and so appeal to different specialist interest groups.

There are also some disadvantages:

- Your article, unless it is published by a third party such as a journal, will not be peer reviewed; academic readers will know this, and journals may feel disinclined to accept work which has already been aired on the internet.
- Your work can be used by others, who may feel less obliged to cite your article if, for example, it was published on an informal research forum.
- Your work might be altered or misappropriated without your knowledge.
- Although you could prove precedence in an area, this is potentially more difficult to do than for an article published in hard copy.
- You can spend a disproportionate amount of time on internet journal articles, to the detriment of peer reviewed publications which would be more beneficial in advancing your career and academic standing.

Despite these possible disadvantages, we would not advocate a refusal even to consider publishing on the internet. We are aware of researchers who, in the early stages of their academic career, have used this resource effectively to promote their reputation. We also know of more established academics who regularly use it to promote discussion around their research. We would simply urge you to consider it in a certain way. As a researcher you are undertaking many tasks, from gathering material to finessing your methodology, from attending research seminars to, perhaps, teaching others. You could see internet writing as similar: something else that you might do to help you to focus your thoughts and develop your ideas, a way to enlarge your support network and discuss developments, but all the while your main focus will remain on your principal writing tasks which might include preparing your thesis or dissertation, preparing conference papers and producing journal articles.

> Publishing an article on the internet could bring advantages, but consider the potential pitfalls before you jump in.

LEAD AUTHOR VS ET AL.

Of course you will expect your name to appear on any jointly authored article you help to produce, but where? At the head, as lead author? As one of several named authors? Or perhaps, in the catalogue, relegated to 'et al.', the term used to denote that several other authors have been involved in addition to the lead author?

The issue of academic authorship is a thorny one in certain areas of intellectual pursuit, some taking the view that the Principal Investigator should be listed as lead author regardless of level of contribution, some feeling that all of those involved in a bid for funding should have their names on resulting articles. Some journals have tried to clarify the situation by setting out guidelines for authors about how they should be listed, if at all, whilst others have taken the decision to list joint authors alphabetically, regardless of level of contribution.

If you are a joint author of an article, this need not be a huge problem. Clearly you do not want to spend years of your academic life as 'et al.', and you will want to be lead author if that is what you are, but in our experience there is only one way to resolve this issue: communication. The earlier in the process you begin a discussion about authorship, the less likely you are to find this problematic.

> If you are jointly producing an article, decide on authorship attribution in the early planning stages of the project.

ACADEMIA VS 'THE PUBLIC'

If your subject area suddenly becomes a 'hot topic' in the news more generally, you may find yourself, with little warning, in the middle of media interest for which you are, understandably, ill prepared. This is an exciting experience. Your research could now reach millions of people but it is also daunting. The media could distort what you are trying to say, or take your research findings out of context to use them in a way in which you had never intended. However confident you feel in your ability to be clear and unequivocal about your research, however firm you are in your resolve, it makes little sense to ignore the support and protection which your institution offers you.

You need protection not just from media outlets which might distort your research, but also from yourself, in that you might inadvertently reveal information which is classified, or commercially sensitive, or claim the right to speak about your material even though it is actually registered as the intellectual property of your institution or a sponsor.

You also, of course, have the members of staff of the journal to support you. They have an interest in the intellectual property rights conferred in your article and will be used to dealing with a wider public interest in the material which they publish.

> See your institution, and your chosen journal, as a protective shield between your work and the vagaries of the general media.

USEFUL WEBSITE

www.publicationethics.org

SOME FINAL THOUGHTS

Now that we have journeyed through this book together you probably know us much better: our views on how to approach journal articles, our thoughts on how to save yourself time and wasted effort whilst still producing a quality article, some of our trials and tribulations in this field, and our determination that you should succeed in this endeavour.

We also feel that we know more about you. By working through this book you are clearly motivated to succeed and you now have the techniques and guidance you need to do this and make it into a positive experience for you. You may have thought, before you opened this book, that all you were going to do was to write a journal article. You will have learnt that the road to success is more demanding, as you plan, design, renegotiate, write and then polish your work. Of course, this also makes it so much more rewarding. Writing a successful article goes beyond merely conveying a message: it is a creative process which challenges you to interrogate your ideas and then search for the best way to persuade readers that your hypothesis is sound and worth exploring. It also requires you to develop skills away from your basic research, those of organising material for publication, writing elegantly and forming a persuasive argument.

By this stage you may well have your article planned, as you worked through each chapter, or perhaps you have been returning to this guide again and again as you came to each new step, in which case it will be written already. Whichever stage you have reached, we know that you have the tools to be a successful writer of articles. We fully expect to see you in print. Good luck!

FURTHER READING

A Concise Dictionary of Confusables by B. A. Pythian (Hodder and Stoughton, 1989, ISBN 978-0340495339)
A very useful book, with clear examples of how confusing words should be used. Although it is old, it has not dated.

Collins Gem English Grammar (Collins, 2006, ISBN 978-0007224210)
Small and easy to carry around with you, but only useful for specific queries. It can be a bit daunting to browse through.

The Mind Map Book by Tony and Barry Buzan (BBC Active, 2009, ISBN 978-1406647167)
This book contains some useful examples of how to use the technique for planning.

Oxford A–Z of Grammar and Punctuation by John Seely (Oxford University Press, 2009, ISBN 978-0199564675)
A marvellous book – really easy to use and covering everything most of us would ever need to know.

MHRA Style Guide (Modern Humanities Research Association, 2008, ISBN 978-0947623760)
A useful guide for keeping your written output consistent, accurate and precise.

The Writers' and Artists' Yearbook (A & C Black Publishers Limited, 2010, ISBN 978-1408124932)
If you would like to glance at inspirational options for a wider audience, this book is for you.

INDEX

abstract 19, 75–7, 92, 111
ambushing yourself 70–2

boredom 61, 69
brainstorming 35–7, 53–6
    brainstorming online 55

career advancement 4, 8, 19, 21, 24, 26, 133
checking 89–94
citations 19
commitment 114
communication 113
conclusion to your article 81
conference papers 7, 12, 15, 17, 23, 64,
    103, 107
confidence 61, 63–4, 69
critical friend 66, 102

dissertation/thesis 3, 12–13
distraction 61, 62–3, 69
draft material 13, 15

editing 86–9, 89–94, 96
editorial board/panel 19, 20, 22, 90, 93, 108–18
ethics 133

feedback 23, 101
flowchart 51–3
focus
    of article 22, 31, 37, 61, 126–7
    loss of 67, 70

general journals 19, 25, 26, 105
global circulation 20, 23, 114, 134
government bodies 21

hierarchical chart 51

ideas 6, 9, 10–11, 28, 43, 126–7
impact 24–7
intellectual property rights (IPR) 22, 106,
    111, 129–37
internet 21, 105, 134–6
introduction to your article 77, 90

joint authoring 10, 55, 136
joint research 15–16, 17, 136

keywords in abstract 76

lead author 136
library 19
list plan 40–1, 48–9, 52

magazines 105, 106
mentor/supervisor 2, 4, 9, 10, 14, 19, 38, 43, 45,
    48, 51, 64, 66, 74, 75, 86–7, 101, 103, 117,
    122, 133
mind mapping 56–8
monograph 5, 8, 10, 26

networking 7, 21, 23
newspapers 105–6

open access 21

page limits 78
patents 133
patience 110
peer review 14, 21, 101, 108–18
personalised timetable 63, 66–7, 69, 71–2

plagiarism 132
planning 7, 8, 25, 30–41, 42–58, 64, 68, 69, 71,
    85, 111, 112
Principal Investigator 133, 136
proof readers 74, 75, 109, 110
psychometric tests 99

readership 5, 11, 13, 14, 17, 31, 33, 82–3, 93, 113
reading aloud 86, 102
recording your words 71
rejection 119–28
    rejection plan 128
Research Assessment Exercise (RAE) 24
research councils 21, 133
Research Excellence Framework (REF) 24–7
research groupings 23, 25, 62, 67
research questions 30, 61–2, 65, 67, 69
research seminars 7, 16, 23, 64, 71, 107,
    115, 124
resilience 115
resource centre 19

second language 74
signposting 79–80, 112
size of article, controlling it 8, 30, 32–4, 44–5,
    64–5, 86–9, 90

source material 12–18, 29, 107, 127–8
specialist issues of journals 20, 23
spider chart 39, 46–51
structure of article 75–82, 111–12, 126–7
supervisor/mentor 2, 4, 9, 10, 14, 19, 38, 43, 45,
    48, 51, 64, 66, 74, 75, 86–7, 101, 103, 117,
    122, 133

target journal 4, 6, 7, 11, 18–24, 29, 52,
    68–9, 105
teaching materials 14, 17–18, 31,
    107, 124
technical data 80–1
technical editors 75, 109
thesis/dissertation 3, 12–13
timing 9–10, 97–8, 128
tiredness 61, 69
translations 21
trickle down chart 51

workload 9–10, 61, 63, 66–7, 69
writer's block 59–72
writing rhythm 11–12, 71–2, 107
writing strategy 10, 66–7
writing style 11, 13, 22, 32, 43–6, 68–9, 70,
    73–94, 113, 125–6